Foreword
EweMove Sales & Lettings

Foreword by EweMove Sales & Lettings

"Outstanding Personal Service Delivered by Local Property Experts"

In the last few years with the advent of new technology and online innovation, there has been an emergence of new start-ups offering a different service to that of traditional high street agents.

EweMove Sales & Lettings combines the best aspects of online with traditional ways of working. Very much focused on outstanding personal 1:1 service delivered by local property experts.

We've lead the way in disrupting the property market.

EweMove is currently the #1 Most Trusted Estate Agent in the UK, thanks to thousands of 5 star customer reviews on the independent review website Trustpilot.

You may think that not all review sites are genuine however, Trustpilot authenticates every review to ensure it's left by a real person.

An agency that customers love with a risk-free Happy Sale Guarantee may seem too good to be true but EweMove has been built with the customer experience at its heart.

We've found that what matters most to sellers and buyers is convenience and flexibility, which means they want an agent who will work around their busy lives including being available for viewings or to answer questions during weekends or evenings, and the ease of booking appointments online or by phone 24/7.

Selling properties on a DIY basis is a risky and potentially costly process. It's key to have a local property expert with in-depth knowledge of the market, who can make sure you get the best possible result and manage the sale from start to finish.

The 39 Steps
To Avoid a House Sale Nightmare!

From the Estate Agent Who Knows How to Sell Houses Fast

By Glenn Ackroyd

Published by
EweMove Sales & Lettings Limited
Updated May 2019

First printed: 2015

Sixth edition: 2019

Published by: EweMove Sales & Lettings Limited
Cavendish House
Littlewood Drive
Cleckheaton
BD19 4TE

www.EweMove.com

Ordering Information:

Special discounts are available on quantity purchases by corporations, associations, industry training providers and others. For details, contact the publisher at the above listed address.

U.K trade bookstores and wholesalers: Please contact our marketing department.

Tel: 01274 888 750
Email: marketing@ewemove.com

ISBN 978-0-9932254-0-6

Dedication

To all of the wonderful team in the Sheep Pen.

Thank you. Without your support and patience, I would
have never achieved my dream.

Contents

Acknowledgements

I would like to thank the Head Shepherds, Shepherdesses, all of the wonderful flock at the EweMove 'Sheep Pen', my editor and ghost writer: Glenn Ackroyd and my family, without whose help this book would never have been completed.

Thank you for your patience, guidance and for your use of the editor's red pen…

Preface

On average, we move home eight times in our lifetime. The process is incredibly stressful. You can be left feeling frustrated, angry and bewildered by the 'dark arts' that are associated with selling your home.

And your allies in this journey whose job it is to lead you blissfully to the promised land of a stress-free sale? Lawyers and Estate Agents! They're regularly ranked as the least trusted professionals…

It's no wonder that you'll be on tenterhooks when it comes to putting your home on the market. And that's precisely the reason why I decided to write this book.

I lift the lid on the world of estate agency and give you the inside track on how agents work. And you'll get lots of useful nuggets about how to present and market your home for success.

Feel free to dip your toe in to pick up tips and ideas when you need them most. It gives you a complete overview of the sales process, right through from how to market your house, choosing the right agent and securing a sale.

So, these are my 39 Steps to avoid a house sale nightmare.

I sincerely hope that in some way they'll help you achieve your goal of selling your home.

The Best Time to Sell Your Home

Selling your home is an extremely emotional and quite stressful time. It's described as being one of the most stressful moments of our lives, alongside death and divorce! Given the amount of money involved and the life-changing event that is going to take place, it's no wonder that house selling and the housing market is a national obsession.

When people come to sell their homes, it's not a decision that they will have taken overnight. It would be based upon a need to move because of an increasing family size, downsizing to a smaller home or relocating for a better lifestyle or job.

Amongst this cocktail of highly charged human emotions, the house seller will have spent a considerable amount of time thinking through their plans to sell, when to put their house on the market and what they plan to do next. The starting point is when to put the house on the market.

People have different opinions as to the best time, but a commonly held belief is that it's always good to market a home at the beginning of spring.

However, if everybody follows this same notion and vast armies of house sellers all descend onto the market at the same time, your house risks being crowded out, because at any one time, there are only a limited number of buyers on the lookout for a new home.

Another question that people ask is "Should I wait until the housing market goes up?"

This often occurs when the market is going through a period of rising prices, fuelled with salacious newspaper headlines promising untold riches from the next housing boom…

The truth is that quite naturally everybody wants to achieve the best price for their house and they don't want to regret having sold it on the cheap. But what you need to remember is that once you've sold a house you're likely to be moving into a new home that in the main, you'll be going on to buy.

If that's the case, then in any possible rising housing market, it will mean that your new home will also go up in price and, generally speaking, there'll be no significant gain to be had by waiting. Quite the contrary, there'll be the loss of lifestyle benefit by delaying any planned move.

It should also be remembered that if the housing market is 'hot', you're more likely to get a number of bidders interested in your property. And there's nothing to suggest that the house may not go for a price well above the original asking price, because ultimately the market will decide the true price of your house on the date that it sells. Albeit a truly great agent will always be able to influence the final sales price you get.

Almost all agents in every town include the phrase "we'll get you the best possible price for your home", but not every agent can get you the best price, simply down to the law of averages. If you ask an agent who uses this phrase in their marketing to value your home, ask them to show you industry, verifiable data to back their claim!

It's generally always the case that you should never wait for the housing market. It can change quite dramatically (as witnessed during the previous Lehman's collapse) and a potential seller should always move when the time is right for them.

This also applies to the time of year during which you're looking to sell. I've already suggested a counter argument to marketing in spring (when limited buyers will have the pick from a flooded market), but the reality is, if you look at any time of year, there are pros and cons. I've set out some of these in the following tables:

Spring (March – May)

Pros	Cons
It's traditionally seen as the best time of year to sell	Lots of people list their property at this time of year creating a crowded marketplace
The clocks have altered allowing for longer days and extended viewing times	The market is flooded with properties with a limited number of buyers
You have a full spring/summer ahead, giving you a long time on the market to sell	Estate agents are at their busiest and may not have time to give you the attention you deserve
Flowers are in bloom and gardens look at their best	By the time your spring house sale completes, you're likely to be buying towards the end of the year

Summer (June – August)

Pros	Cons
The long summer days give you the opportunity for early evening viewings	Children will be off school and the neighbouring houses could be noisy during viewings
The hot weather allows you to present your home with open French windows, leading out to beautiful gardens	During August, viewings tend to slow down because families are away on holiday
The lovely blue skies enable you to get fantastic exterior photographs	Once you sell a house listed in summer, you're likely to be buying and moving during late winter

Autumn (September – November)

Pros	Cons
In September children are back at school and people are looking to move forward with their house buying plans	At the end of October, the clocks go back resulting in dark, dreary nights
It's generally seen as the last good opportunity to sell a house before Christmas	As leaves fall and flowers die, gardens lose their 'Wow' factor and look unappealing
Any house sellers that have sold in the early part of spring will now be looking to buy	Grey dull skies do not present houses in the best light
You'll have less competition compared to those who place their house on the market in the spring rush	The reducing daylight starts to limit the options for evening viewings

Winter (December – February)

Pros	Cons
January is generally a good time to put properties on the market	Some people do not wish to move or make plans before Christmas
After Christmas, regrettably there are lots of relationship breakdowns resulting in people having to move	Dark nights do not favour evening viewings
Marketing a property early, allows you to beat the spring rush and face less competition from other house sellers	Cold weather and snow can create the perception that your home is cold if it's not well heated throughout

Top Tip!

As you can see from these tables, there are lots of benefits and reasons why every time of year has both good and bad points.

That's why I'll always recommend to a client that they should choose a time that's right for them and not try and manufacture the listing to fit in with the housing market.

Step 2

Kerb Appeal

The saying goes that first impressions last. And you only get one chance to make a first impression…

There's also a belief within the industry that buyers make their decision on whether to buy within 10 seconds of arriving at your home. I believe that this is too simplistic, but the reality is that when your potential buyer arrives, if they have a bad first impression you're starting off on the back foot.

You'll then have an enormous amount of work to do to try and regain the lost momentum and move the prospect into a position of wanting to make you an offer. The problem faced by most people when they come to sell their home is that they fail to see what's under their noses. Indeed, because of familiarity, they often fail to smell what's under their noses! This can include odours from pets that home owners have long become desensitised to. So, when you try to sell your home, you should first try and look dispassionately at your house through the eyes of an observer seeing it for the first time. This is often harder than it seems and you may need to enlist the help of a trusted friend who you can call upon to seek their advice and tell you the brutal truth!

Ask them; "If I absolutely had to sell my house and you needed to help me in the best way that you can - what should I do to make the first impression that a buyer receives as amazing as possible?"

At the end of the day, it's simply a matter of common sense, a bit of good old elbow grease and a few quid spent. All of which will dramatically enhance and improve the presentation of your property upon arrival.

I've produced a handy checklist for you to use as a guide:

Preparing Your Home

Clear the garden of any children's toys/trampolines etc.	
Clear the garage/shed of any junk/items that you will not be taking to your new home	
Weed the garden and sweep up any leaves	
Jet wash any pathways and driveways	
Repair any broken fences and gates	
Paint any exterior woodwork and metalwork, for example gates, fences, gutters and doors	
Clear gutters and make sure that the roof has no missing or damaged tiles	
Clean windows inside and out	
Plant seasonal flowers and/or hanging baskets	
On the day of the viewing make sure that the driveway or roadside is clear for the viewer to park their car	
Try to conduct your viewings during the day	
If your property has two entrances, guide them to the entrance that has the most scenic visual outlook	

These steps just cover the exterior of your property and my next few steps will help you deal with the inside of your home.

A good way to look for inspiration on how to improve the appearance of your property is to get ideas from the best houses on your street and copy what they've done.

But what if you find yourself in a situation where your house looks immaculate, but it's being let down by a neighbouring property? Sometimes, the house next door can be extremely off putting to potential buyers. Remember, they're not just buying a house, they're also forming an opinion on their possible future neighbours.

Most people assume that nothing can be done in these situations, but if you're determined to get a sale and want the best price, you can take the initiative.

I know one particular owner who had a house next to a property that had an overgrown garden, litter strewn outside and a tired broken fence. It looked horrendous and was a complete eyesore.

The neighbours were elderly and sadly unable to maintain their property. So, the seller approached them and offered to do all the clearance work. For a few hundred pounds and a weekend's hard graft, the front garden was transformed. They'd dramatically improved their chances of a sale and at the same time performed a good deed for their extremely grateful neighbours. The story had a happy ending with the seller achieving the full asking price in a matter of weeks.

Step 3

De-clutter and Clean

Imagine for one day you've turned into Mrs Hinch or you're a dedicated member of the Hinch Army! (For those who are not aware of Mrs Hinch, Sophie Hinchcliffe has become an online sensation after sharing cleaning hacks on Instagram.)

Start to think of what Mrs Hinch would do if she got her hands on your home. This is where you need to start, this will more than likely be removing built-up clutter to allow you to complete a thorough clean.

It's amazing how dirty our homes become and you'll soon find out as you begin to work through this step and implement my handy checklist.

You need to place yourself in the shoes of your buyer. When they come into your home, full of its treasures and nick-knacks, they don't picture a house full of character. All they'll see is a space that's crowded full of somebody else's items. This makes it difficult for someone to imagine themselves living there. You need to overcome this barrier because by doing so it will help you sell your house quickly and make your onward move much simpler. Give away or re-cycle, anything that you're not going to take with you to your new home - NOW!

Start with this golden rule...

We're all guilty of hoarding items that may be broken (which one day we intend to repair...), or have long since ceased to be of any use (those VHS videos and old record players!). They tend to lurk under beds, in storage cupboards, in garages and the attic. Remember the time when these were once handy storage spaces? But now they've morphed into junkyard storage monsters.

I find the best way of tackling this is head on, in one fell swoop. This involves setting aside a weekend to travel to and from the local council waste disposal or recycling site. It's actually quite liberating and very cathartic!

You must make sure that you throw away all items that are broken. If your potential buyer sees something that's not working, subconsciously they'll be thinking; "What else in this house needs fixing and how much is it going to cost me?"

When doing this, don't forget to attack the kitchen cupboards. They hold a treasure trove of out of date tins of food and long since forgotten ingredients. Remember the ones you bought for the cookbook recipe that you received as a present? You used it once, before putting it back on the bookshelf, never to see daylight again...

You should also throw away any chipped or broken cups, crockery and pans. One of the key places that your buyer will look will be your kitchen and they'll want to open the cupboard doors. You need to make sure when they do, they'll find a nice orderly selection of items, with plenty of additional space for further items (for when they receive their cookbook as a present).

What you don't want is for them to open a cupboard and have to duck to avoid a jar of Bisto hurtling towards them. You know the one. You put it on top of a tin of soup and it's been waiting until now to choose the perfect moment to make its bid for freedom…

When it comes to cleaning your home, there are certain things that you will do on every occasion before a viewer arrives. For example:

1. Vacuuming

2. Putting away clothes and unloading the washing machine

3. Emptying the dishwasher

4. Tidying rooms

But there are certain "deep cleaning" items that you need to tackle head on before you can put the property on the market. This is to make sure that it's shipshape and ready for when your buyers arrive. And remember, as soon as your property goes live online, it's likely that you'll get the most interest straight away, so there's no time to wait.

On the next page, there's a handy checklist for you to work through in terms of your cleaning regime before you're ready to sell.

Now this may all seem like a lot of hard work, and it's very easy to put it off until you get your first viewing. I've been guilty of doing this, only to find that when the buyer arrives, there's simply no time. The fact is that a couple of days of hard work can quite literally add thousands of pounds to your house value and help you ensure that the sale goes through quickly. It will be time and money extremely well spent and when it comes to moving into your new home, all the items that you've thrown out along the way will make the move far easier.

If you don't have time to do this yourself think about hiring a local cleaner to do a one-off deep clean for you.

Once done, you can sit back and relax with your favourite tipple! You can also enjoy your 'new' home and all its extra space for the remaining few months until it's finally sold, satisfied with a job well done.

Wash down all window frames and clean windows inside and out.	
Wash around light fittings and scrape off any wall paint.	
Wash down all woodwork including skirting boards.	
Clean window blinds.	
Re-grout and re-whiten all tiles in the kitchen, bathroom and WCs.	
Remove any personal hygiene items from the bathroom. Nobody likes to see a used toothbrush, toothpaste or razor when they are viewing someone else's home!	
Make sure that the house is clean, paying particular attention to the bathroom and kitchen. These rooms should be washed down with lemon fresh bleach, leaving a nice fragrance.	
Vacuum the house.	
Wash/deep clean carpets. A good tip is to hire a professional carpet cleaner. B&Q and other outlets provide these for around £30 per weekend. These are great for reducing pet smells but hiring a professional carpet cleaning firm is also well worth the cost.	
Clean all of your kitchen appliances. The kitchen is the most important room in the house and your buyers will open up your dishwasher and ovens and look inside. It's vital that these appliances are spotless!	

Step 4

Repair and Decorate

When the time comes to sell and you're looking at inviting those evil estate agents around, you'll be wondering whether it's worth the investment and cost of repairing and decorating your home. You may consider this to be a wasted expense given that the new buyers may want to change the home according to their own personal taste. You can ask estate agents for advice and in almost every case you'll get the reply that you should market the home as it is because it's impossible to know the requirements of your potential purchaser.

Frankly, I don't buy into this school of thought. Estate agents are trained to sign up customers on the spot. They know that giving the client any chance to take time out and think about their decision, such as going away and doing home improvements, is an opportunity for that vendor to go to another agent. For this reason, you must question whether an agent is giving you the best advice to sell the home as is, or advice which suits their particular agenda of signing you up on the spot…

Now don't get me wrong, there are instances when it's right to market your home as is, for example if the house is a "fixer upper". That's when a house is in need of significant improvement works, such that it will only be attractive to builders or private investors as a renovation project. On these occasions, the cost of making good the property will be substantial and it may not be practical or financially feasible for you to consider. But the majority of buyers are simply looking for a home that they can move into straight away. Their budgets are likely to be limited and they may not have the skills or inclination to embark upon a DIY project.

To give you another perspective, consider it from the point of view of a new housing developer. Do they build a house, put in all the walls and kitchen, but then leave it undecorated, without carpets and unfurnished? Do they worry that the buyer will want to change it to create their own vision of an ideal home? Obviously not! They know from years of experience and hundreds of millions of pounds of sales, that presenting a "show home" works. One with nice neutral colours, simple decoration and the illusion of lots of space. This helps them sell and more importantly gets them the best asking price.

So, I remain of the very firm opinion that it's almost always in the best interests of a client to do whatever reasonable works can be done to make the house shipshape and ready for sale.

Remember that the buyers looking around your home are going to be taking a very keen interest in every minor detail. Anything that's not in working order or requires repair, is going to flag up in their minds as another cost. It's going to present itself as a problem which they'll have to deal with at some point. Some buyers may be happy, but having a house with outstanding repairs or in poor decoration, is going to significantly limit the number of potential offers.

Quite simply, the more interested parties you have, the quicker your house will sell and the higher the price you're likely to get for it.

This does not mean that you have to decorate your house from top to bottom. Look for certain areas that may need freshening up. Heavy duty places such as a living room, dining room or stairways are often parts of your home that get the odd marking and discolouration from use. When you are considering redecorating, you can get a lot of inspiration and ideas by visiting a few new build housing developments near you. Spend a day one weekend checking out how they've presented their show homes.

And keep in mind; your home may not need a full makeover. The rule here is - keep it as simple as possible.

Here's my handy guide on how to decorate your home by keeping it neutral:

1. **Ceilings – Matt white.** This brightens the room, creating the illusion of more space and light

2. **Walls – Very pale grey.** It's bright and simple, cool and contemporary which easily blends with other colours.

3. **Woodwork and skirtings – White gloss.** It's clean, bright and complements the room

4. **Carpet – Pale grey.** This makes the room look light and bright and is consistent with the neutral colour scheme. Remember that a light-coloured carpet easily picks up dirt, so you must take off your shoes at all times. This is only a short-term measure until the house is sold.

The cost of getting the paint and doing the work yourself will be relatively inexpensive. And you can significantly enhance the appearance of your home and its value. It might seem a bit of a challenge, but ask yourself this; "Are you prepared to spend a couple of weekends to potentially achieve the equivalent amount of money that could pay for an incredible family holiday?"

This could, quite literally be the amount of extra money you'll get by securing a higher sale price.

You should also read the next step relating to Home Staging, which introduces professionals who can assist you with this area of work.

Step 5

Home Staging

Home make over shows on TV have brought to the nation the idea that, with a little inspiration, our homes can be transformed into a designers dream. And all in a couple of days… It all looks oh so simple!

You might lament that the dream of a 'designer home' is only the preserve of the rich. Who else can afford to pay for such extravagant consultants? Well, hold that thought and let me introduce to you an alternative, which can be relatively inexpensive and achieve strikingly similar results. Home Staging has been around for a number of years and even has its own association; the Academy of British Home Stagers.

There are a small number of providers in the UK, who you can easily find by searching online for "home stagers". They offer a range of services including:

Home Consultation

This involves a Home Stager specialist meeting you at your home, ascertaining your needs and then coming up with a Design Report and plan to meet with your requirements. This is likely to include setting out advice and giving direction on wallpaper or paint colourings and a schedule of the works to be done. They'll then usually offer an additional service to source and/or arrange for tradesmen to carry out the works should you so wish.

You can simply pay for the consultation and report and arrange for the works to be done by yourself. This means that you get all the benefit of the designer's eye in terms of matching the correct wall and ceiling colours, together with carpets and furnishings etc. So when the complete picture comes together, everything is perfectly coordinated. This gives you the confidence to go out and do the work, by simply following the step-by-step design template.

Depending upon the extent of the project and how much work you want to be done thereafter, the initial consultation and report tends to cost around £300-500. Obviously if you go on to engage the Home Stager with the project management, the cost will be greater.

Project Management

This can be limited to simply providing you with a list of contractors and enabling you to arrange the works yourself, or going the full way through to the Home Stager actually instructing the works and overseeing them, to make sure that they are completed as planned. This may mean that they are sourcing supplies from wholesalers, as well as making sure the relevant tradesman are working together. Depending upon the nature and size of the project, the cost of this can be in the order of a few thousand pounds.

If you are considering project management, you'll need to weigh up the cost against the potential added value that a professional designer can provide in terms of increasing the likely sale price.

Furniture Rental

This service is mainly utilised by housing developers and builders. Professional Home Stagers can supply a complete house of furnishings right through from sofas and dining chairs to appliances and place them into a property. They are normally charged on a monthly rental until the house is sold.

As detailed in Step 4, housing developers know that showcasing a perfect home, presented nicely, helps them to achieve top dollar. That's why they'll go the extra mile and invest money by renting items in order to help them secure the best price.

I know one house seller who used a Home Staging company to simply provide the basic consultation and a Design Report. He used this to go out and source the paint and materials and then arranged to get the work done himself. This cost him under £300 and he was able to create his own version of a 'show home' at an extremely modest cost.

I also know a couple that engaged a Home Stager to furnish their own home. It was a large five-bedroom property that had been completely renovated. The project initially involved coming up with a design concept to choose the colouring for the walls and carpets in each room, the rugs, the curtains, tiles, even down to the lighting and door furniture. It included sourcing all the materials from a multitude of different suppliers and then arranging the works with a variety of different tradesmen spanning six months. The report and project management cost approximately £7,000. Upon completion, the house had increased in value by £25,000.

As you can see, you can achieve amazing results by spending as little as a few hundred, right through to several thousand pounds. It all depends upon the extent of works and your budget.

To find out more about Home Staging, you can check out these websites:

1.   www.homestagers.co.uk (consultation, project management and rental)

2.   www.housewow.co.uk (consultation, project management and rental)

3.   www.davidphillips.com (specialists in providing furniture rental, particularly for high-end developers)

Step 6

Pets

If you have pets, you'll love them to bits and they'll be part of the family. So, a word of warning here. You may not like me for some of the blunt advice in this section! (But I love pets too…)

One of the problems that we all face with our pets is that they have their own particular smells and, as homeowners we get used to them. So, we become desensitised and the smell of our home is, to all intents and purposes, 'normal'. To potential buyers, who'll be unfamiliar with your pet's particular pong, this may well be off putting to say the least. It's for this reason within Step 3 – 'De-clutter and Clean', that I recommend that you wash your carpets with a professional cleaner.

And of course, some potential buyers will love your pets. But remember that your job when selling your home is to try and make it appeal to the widest possible audience. So, you don't want to alienate any potential buyers along the way. That includes people who may not like certain animals or indeed who may be allergic to them.

And please understand that I'm not suggesting that you get rid of your pets! What I'm trying to suggest is that it would be in your best interests to minimise the impact of your pet on potential viewers by following a few simple rules: –

1. If you have dogs, make sure that any mess or fouling is completely removed from the garden (Yuck!)

2. If you have feeding bowls, make sure they are removed from the kitchen during viewings. At the very least move them to a utility room or other area where no food is prepared.

3. Remove cat litter trays or make sure they are emptied.

4. When viewings are being conducted, where possible, arrange for your pets be away from the property. Put your cats out and take your dog for a walk.

Now having carried out this advice, 'Sod's Law' will mean that your perfect buyer will be a pet lover, who'll also have the same animal as you. As a result, you'll instantly strike up a rapport and they'll fall in love with your home and buy it. At which point, you can call me and tell me that I don't have a clue what I'm talking about!

Step 7

Photographs

The saying goes that; "a picture paints a thousand words" and it's never been truer than when it comes to selling your home.

This section is perhaps the most vital in this book when it comes to success in selling your home.

Let's consider why.

Your prospective buyer's journey is likely to start out with a search on a property portal, such as Rightmove or Zoopla. They'll enter their search criteria and typically up will pop ten listings. Each will show a very short description and a thumbnail sized photograph. Rightmove's own studies show that house buyers will spend on average 1 minute per property on the details, 48 seconds when they click on photos and 55 seconds on average on floorplans.

That's only a very small window of opportunity for your property to stand out and shine and the biggest single factor in this decision is the photograph. You could have the best marketing description in the world, incredible photographs inside, but unless your elusive buyer has clicked through to see the details, you'll fall down at the first hurdle...

In the US, the National Association of Realtors carried out a study. It revealed that online listings with professional photography generated an average of 61% more page views.

Just to explain further, 'professional photography', is not your run-of-the-mill estate agency photography. This study was specifically carried out and measured in respect of DSLR cameras. That's the technical term for cameras with detachable lenses.

The key differentiator with DSLR cameras is the ability to have wide-angle lenses that enable the photographer to capture a wider field of view when taking internal photographs. This means that more of your room is displayed, giving the impression of a bigger room size. This makes sure that the buyer is not left with the mistaken belief that your rooms are smaller than they actually are.

When choosing an estate agent, it's crucial that you find out whether or not they've been professionally trained at a Property Photography Academy. All EweMove branch directors receive their training from one of the industry's leading photography experts:

www.propertyphotographyacademy.co.uk

External Photographs

In view of the importance of the first picture, which is the main one shown on a portal search, it's vital that it looks amazing. So when you're taking this front view picture, you should remove any cars from the driveway, dustbins and unsightly children's toys. Where possible, you should aim to take the shot on a nice sunny day with a beautiful clear blue sky.

Given the British weather, unfortunately this is not always possible. But a good estate agent will be able to insert a blue sky as a backdrop. I'm able to do this using my editing software (you can also use packages like Photoshop). If a house seller in my area wants to replace their current poor photographs with professional ones, I provide a free service for exterior shots. I'm even happy to do this if the house is listed with another agent.

There really is no excuse for estate agents taking poor photographs because you can now even use online suppliers to edit them for you for as little as £4. For an example of one such provider, check out:

www.myphotogenie.co.uk

Online photo editors can do a whole range of things including removing dustbins, cars and 'For Sale' boards. Remember, you cannot remove anything that is a fixture of the property, such as a nearby lamppost or electricity pylon! Only movable items can be edited out.

The key to taking good photographs is to take lots of them. You can then select the best ones later. When taking exterior photographs, make sure that you take them from an angle and if needs be, from an elevated position.

But despite all of what I've said so far, almost every listing that your potential buyer will search through will look pretty much the same. Reams and reams of house fronts, boring angles, boring views... How can you make yours really stand out from the crowd?

The key to this is to try and be different. For example, if you have a large home, like a five bedroom property, this is likely to appeal to a family.

You may have a picture of all the family lined up in size order smiling outside to demonstrate it's a family home. It's quirky, different and will draw your viewer's eye.

Another example would be to have a picture of a beautiful looking door and have the marketing description saying, "What's on the other side of this door? You'll be astonished when you find out…" Curiosity killed the cat and will suck in your nosey buyer…

One of my colleagues had the great idea of using a drawing done by the seller's child as the main photograph. It even had his name and age on so that it could be proudly shared on Facebook! Obviously, it was a child's drawing, but it stood out. People warmed to the idea and it got a far higher click through rate as a result.

If none of these options are available you could always use an alternative picture, such as fantastic feature room like the kitchen or living room. Or what about a patio table set out with plates, wine glasses and scrummy food on a summers day?

Internal Photographs

When it comes to internal photographs, you should take wide-angle photos of as many rooms as possible, because your buyer will spend a lot of time browsing online before they decide to book a viewing.

As a general rule, Rightmove recommend between 8-10 internal photographs for a standard 2-3 bed home. Obviously, the amount will increase if it's a very large home or if it has lots of jaw-dropping features that you want to show off. A large home may have 15-20 photos. But that should be your limit!

The aim of your photos is not to present a virtual tour of every room in your home, removing the need for a potential buyer to view. It's to tempt and arouse their interest by showcasing your very best rooms. The teaser photos should leave them wanting more… And to get more, they'll need to arrange a viewing. This is the point at which they can be moved towards making an offer.

When taking photos, remember that this is going to be your key marketing weapon when selling your home. Your photographs are going to be your brochure to the online world. You should imagine that you have received a call from a lifestyle magazine that wants to feature your property as this month's centrefold. How would you present your home, given that it's going to be viewed by a large audience and you want to impress?

Don't just present the rooms based upon regurgitating a list of boring features. The person who is buying your home is acquiring a lifestyle and wants to visualise it as a lovely warm cosy home that they and their family are going to enjoy. A good tip is to ensure that you take photographs when there is lots of natural light and all the curtains are fully drawn with blinds open.

You should get fresh flowers for the living room/kitchen, fresh fruit, have lighted tea lights and even set the dining table with your best crockery and cutlery. You can even go as far as having a bottle of wine on display, wine glasses out and a salad bowl. All of this helps paint a picture of a lovely welcoming home in which to rest, relax, eat and enjoy.

When it comes to the kitchen, it should be spotless and other than electrical appliances, there should be nothing left out on the worktops. Your bathroom should be gleaming and free from any personal toiletries. Have some flowers on display and complement the room with nicely folded, colour-coordinated hand towels, together with hand wash/lotion accessories etc.

Hopefully this step will have given you some pointers, but don't be afraid to ask your estate agent to come back and retake photographs if you're not happy with them. The importance of fantastic photographs cannot be overstated when it comes to selling your home. This is the one thing that you need to spend time and effort getting right; to make sure that your home is presented in the best way possible.

Top Tip!

If your property is listed for sale with another agent and you don't think that your main photo does your property justice, simply contact me by email (my details are on the back of this book). I'll be delighted to take a set of professional shots and email them to you for your agent to use, completely free of charge.

Step 8

Getting Floor Plans

Second only to brilliant photographs, floor plans are absolutely essential when it comes to marketing your home properly. Once your buyer has reviewed your online details and spent their time flicking through each and every picture, ordinarily their next port of call is to examine in great detail the floor plans displayed on the online portal. They'll do this before making the decision of whether or not to book a viewing. And there's good reason. They need to make sure that the size of the house and, in particular key areas such as bedrooms, meet with their requirements.

For example, a couple looking for a 3-bed property may need to make sure that a certain number of the bedrooms will fit a double bed. They can quickly find this information from a good floor plan and this will save them and you the time and trouble of a potentially wasted viewing. Metropix, a leading UK provider of floor plans for estate agents, state that properties with floor plans generate 30% more interest. This means more enquiries and will hopefully result in a faster sale at a better price.

Your estate agent should provide floor plans as part of their normal service, free of charge. One thing that you need to make sure of is that you are not settling for a bog standard, basic 2D floor plan. I always make sure that when providing floor plans for my clients, they receive both 2D and 3D plans.

3D plans allow the house to be 'brought to life' by creating a brilliant visual presentation, including furnishings etc. The potential buyer is better able to see themselves living in the home and how the space can be utilised. Don't settle for anything less!

You must also make sure that the floor plans include measurements. These should be in both metric and imperial format. This will allow people to have a clear understanding of the size of rooms in comparison to their current home.

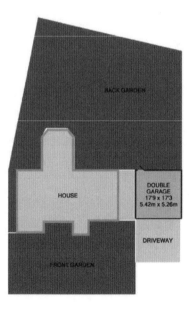

Your agent should also have the ability to show a plan of the house, including gardens.

Agents seem to forget that gardens, their location in relation to the sun and the size of the land that comes with the home is vital information.

A simple plan like you see to the left makes it perfectly clear that this house has extensive gardens and will encourage would be buyers to take action. It also shows that there is ample parking with the double garage.

The same house with 2D plan:

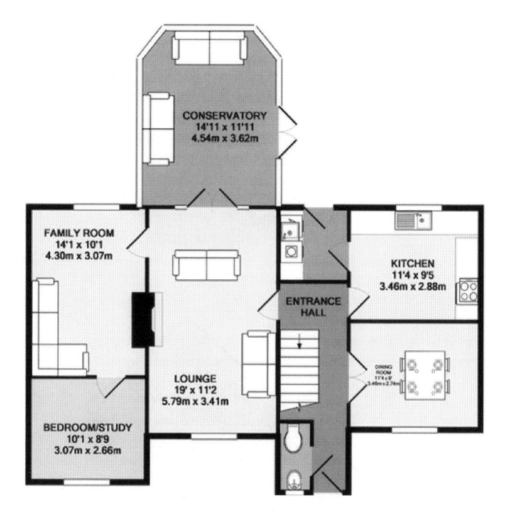

CONSERVATORY
14'11 x 11'11
4.54m x 3.62m

FAMILY ROOM
14'1 x 10'1
4.30m x 3.07m

KITCHEN
11'4 x 9'5
3.46m x 2.88m

ENTRANCE
HALL

LOUNGE
19' x 11'2
5.79m x 3.41m

DINING
ROOM
11'4 x 9'
3.46m x 2.74m

BEDROOM/STUDY
10'1 x 8'9
3.07m x 2.66m

The same house in 3D:

Marketing Description

After superb photographs and 2D/3D floor plans, the final instalment in the estate agent's holy trinity of 'must haves' is a seductive marketing description.

One thing that needs to be pointed out from the off is that all marketing statements must be true. You cannot claim to have a bedroom when in reality it doesn't have a window. There are strict rules governing what can and can't be said, which are set out in the Consumer Protection from Unfair Trading Regulations (2008) and the Business Protection from Misleading Marketing Regulations (2008), (which replaced the Property Misdescriptions Act 1991). This means that all room measurements must be true and the rooms must be as described.

Where most estate agents fall down with their marketing is that they spew a boring list of rooms, their measurements and all the internal fittings, such as radiators, without actually doing what they are being paid to do. And that's selling their client's home!

A property description should paint a lifestyle by including evocative and descriptive words, creating a beautiful picture for the potential buyer. Upon reading, they should be able to see themselves living there blissfully in their perfect welcoming home…

When starting a marketing description, you should cover all of the basics, such as listing the rooms and any key features. You don't need to go overboard and list details like light fittings, or the fact that every room has a radiator. Work from the bottom of the house, up through each floor and don't forget to include front and rear gardens, garages and outbuildings. Of course, you must include measurements in both metric and imperial.

Then you need to think to yourself "What in this house makes it special and would stop a buyer in their tracks and go WOW!?" Things to include may be a stunning feature fireplace, a relaxing spa bath that's simply joyous to use, an amazing conservatory which allows you to bathe in the sunshine, or a luxury kitchen which will make you the envy of all of your friends…

Don't try to list features from every room, only say your top 5. Then make a point of describing them in glowing terms. You should consider using powerful adjectives like "delicious", "cosy", "adorable", "relaxing" and "delightful" etc. but please be mindful of the audience you are appealing to. Imagine yourself crafting a Marks & Sparks Belgian chocolate pudding advert, but for your home.

This is no ordinary home; this is quite possibly the finest property that you'll find on the market… You get the picture! Swiftly moving on…

The key to this is making sure that your initial 300 characters, which are the ones that appear in the summary listing on the portal, are the most compelling and appealing to your would-be buyer. Forget the boring "a good sized three bed semi-detached…". This is your one chance to shine and grab your buyers' interest. Don't miss out on the opportunity! Here are some good examples:

- A charming character cottage, neatly tucked away in this delightful village hamlet

- Quite possibly the finest family home on the market right now

- Welcome to your perfect dream home

- Does this home have the best view in the County? Decide for yourself

This principle can be applied when setting out the further description and highlighting certain rooms such as living rooms, kitchen or conservatories. For example:

- Imagine yourself on a winter's evening, with snow in the garden, sitting in front of the "real flame" fire, warm and cosy whilst sipping a glass of your favourite wine after a long, hard day...

- Picture you and your family sitting in the homely kitchen, enjoying your favourite Sunday roast, whilst putting the world to rights...

- You can relax and unwind during a summer evening, whilst enjoying a delicious barbecue, taking full advantage of the patio area, which will be the envy of your friends and neighbours

- Relax, unwind and let your troubles melt away in this luxury spa bath, which would not be out of place in the finest 5 Star hotel

A word of warning

I do see lots of agents who simply churn out template descriptions listing a bland set of characterless features. Given the importance of your marketing description, don't be afraid to challenge your estate agent and indeed re-write the description until you're happy with it. Remember, this is your property and the amount of money involved is substantial, so you need to get it right.

Top Tip!

On the portals' Summary Listings, Rightmove or Zoopla will display the first 300 characters of your description. You must use compelling text to grab hold of your buyers' attention and make sure that you stand out from the rest of the mundane listings.

Step 10

Brochures

Traditionally estate agents would produce property brochures and have them on display in shop front windows and hand them out to people who were interested. They would even get photographs developed on 35mm film and hand glue them onto the printed brochures.

Thankfully times have moved on and most house hunters browse online in the evening, or at weekends rather than visiting traditional branches.

That's the reason why photographs, floor plans and the property description are so important as outlined in Steps 7, 8 and 9.

It's for this reason that I do not recommend that my clients go to the expense of having professional brochures produced. People can quite easily print them off from Rightmove and Zoopla etc. Good estate agency websites, including our own at ewemove.com, provide professionally designed templates that can be easily downloaded as a PDF. Quality brochures can be printed out on high quality print paper and look perfect when handed out at viewings.

There are a few exceptions to this. If you have a high-end luxury or prestige home, which in turn commands a very high price tag, then paying a few hundred pounds to have an extremely well-polished brochure is a good sales tool. But for the vast majority of homes, the expense is not justified.

You should be cautious when any estate agent tries to push this service to you, because they may be doing so in order to generate some extra fees, rather than trying to serve your best interests.

Step 11

Getting Your Market Appraisal

Before you embark upon the daunting prospect of inviting a number of estate agents into your home, it's a good idea to do your own research to get a feel for what your house is worth. Often, you'll have a good sense for your home's value because of your awareness of properties that have come onto the market and sold in the previous months.

You can look on the main portals such as Rightmove and Zoopla and do a search of similar houses in your area, but bear in mind; these will show current market asking prices. The price achieved is often a little lower than the asking price.

There are websites that provide historic sales data like:

www.ourproperty.co.uk
www.nethouseprices.com

The Nationwide also provides a service that allows you to put in your house price based upon when you bought it, it then gives an adjusted value calculated upon house price changes to the current date. You can try this yourself at:

www.nationwide.co.uk/about/house-price-index/house-price-calculator

I have a tool on my website which provides a free instant online valuation. This is determined by looking at house sales in the immediate area of your home and then adjusting for house price increases. It provides a valuation estimate based upon the comparable data. You can try it yourself now:

www.ewemove.com

Hometrack provides the UK's most accurate automated valuation report. The Automated Valuation Model (AVM) is used by 13 out of the top 15 UK mortgage lenders and supports 80% of mortgage lending in this country! So just as it's important to understand what your credit file says about your financial history, it's equally as important to understand what a Hometrack's AVM report says about your house when you're looking to sell. That's because your buyers mortgage lender is likely to be using it.

This level of industry knowledge is normally the preserve of the big banks. Fortunately, I'm in the lucky position to be part of the UK wide EweMove network, which gives me insider access. I carry out these reports as part of my service to customers, so that they can have this vital information to hand.

If you would like to receive a Hometrack AVM report, please contact me. You can find out how to get your free report at the back of this book.

What you must remember with all computer-aided models is that they are only an estimate and do not constitute a surveyor's valuation. Even when an estate agent comes around and suggests to you a figure to market your property, that does not constitute a valuation. It's simply a marketing guide. Valuations can only be carried out by RICS qualified surveyors who'll charge you handsomely for the privilege. When you have mustered up the courage to call a number of estate agents, you'll no doubt be keen to get an idea of their fees. This is where you need to be aware of the standard industry tricks that are designed to trap you!

Estate agents are trained from birth not to tell you their fees over the phone. They'll make up a heap of excuses like; "I need to see your home fully before I'm able to discuss the fees and what rate I can give to you" This is code for "I want to get in front of you and bore you to death until such time as you sign on the dotted line. Then I've got you trapped on my long-term contract".

Here's another trick from the sneaky estate agent's tool kit. They'll ask you if you've got any other agents coming around and when those appointments are. They'll then try and book themselves in as the last appointment. The reason? By going last, they work on the assumption that they can find out from you what the other agents have valued the house for, and then pitch their suggested sale price higher/or commission rate slightly lower. They'll then rely on the owner's greed and gullibility to snare them.

The final trick is coming around to your home and asking questions like "Do you have any idea what the home is worth?", or "Have any estate agents given you a market appraisal? What did they say?" Upon getting the answer they will nod knowingly (not having carried out their own proper research), and suggest quite confidently that they can beat that price and get you more money...

The sting in the tail is what I call the "estate agency trap". The plucky agent will whip out of their bag a shiny contract and fake Mont Blanc pen. Having promised the earth, they'll sign you up to a long-term contract that you'll struggle to get out of.

If the agent has over valued the property and it doesn't sell quickly, they're likely to contact you and ask you to lower the price. This is to make sure that they can achieve a sale before the minimum contract term has expired. You should be aware that if the contract has been signed at your home, you do have a 14-day cooling off period. If you change your mind, don't be afraid to use this. When obtaining your market appraisals, I'd always advise a customer to get two or three valuations. This enables you to get a range of opinions and it gives you the opportunity to check that the valuer will be the same person actually selling your home and conducting the viewings. You may ask why this is important?

Well, at viewings a skilled and experienced valuer will be able to negotiate the best price for your home there and then because they understand your circumstances and they know everything about your property. You don't want a part-time office junior turning up at your home to do viewings, chances are they won't know anything about your home or circumstances!

Never feel pressured to sign and don't get yourself tied into a long-term contract. If the agent is prepared to put their money where their mouth is and they are confident that they can find you a buyer quickly, you can put them to the challenge by insisting that they have a very short-term contract. Because if they are as good as they say they are, why should they have any objection?

When it comes to making the choice of agent, the only advice I can give here is that you should trust your instincts as to whether or not you believe the agent you are talking to. A Property Academy Home Moving Trends 2017 survey recorded that 78% of customers chose their agent based upon the person that they instinctively liked and trusted.

That person being local, so that they can know the local area, parks, schools etc., enabling them to relate to potential viewers, helped to support this. As the saying goes, when it comes to choosing, ultimately you'll have to 'trust your gut instinct'.

Another tip is to speak to friends and family who may have sold their homes recently. If they have sold and have had a good or bad experience, it will help you make your decision.

One thing that you must not do is to be tempted to go for a marketing price that is markedly above the market value. In the long run, it is likely to be counter-productive. See Step 13 'Pitching Your House Price.'

Top Tip!

Before getting an agent to value your home, do your own research. See my special offer to provide a free Hometrack AVM report, worth £19.95 at the back of this book.

Step 12

Customer Service

The poor reputation held by some estate agents has been forged over many years and a key part of this boils down to the poor customer service reputation that they hold. In the Property Academy Home Moving Trends of 2017, 78% of sellers said that their decision to choose an agent was based upon the one who they liked and trusted could give the best customer service.

A key message from the survey findings was that communication between the agent and the client was at the heart of the customer service experience. The survey found the following:

* 86% of sellers didn't choose the cheapest agent
* 80% of sellers believe technology is important
* 52% of sellers weren't confident to use the same agent again to sell their property

The problem of course lies in the way in which estate agents typically conduct their business. Initially you'll be seen by a valuer who is the slick sales person who brings home the bacon in terms of signed up instructions for the branch.

They'll then throw the paperwork onto the desk of an office junior/ administrator. Their job is to type up the template marketing description for the portals. This person has never set foot in your home and is often not able, or experienced enough, to create a vibrant description that will sell your home by painting a seductive picture.

Calls will then come into the office from potential buyers (only during working hours) and various people will handle them, none of whom know the inside of your home. All they'll be able to offer is a re-reading of the words from their website in a monosyllabic fashion.

When it comes to doing the viewings, lots of estate agents allow you to fend for yourself or will send a random assortment of people from the office to accompany the viewing – we call them 'glorified key-holders'!

When you then seek to get an update as to what's going on, or feedback from viewers, nobody from the plethora of people in the office has the full picture. You're either passed from pillar to post, or left with half a tale. It's no wonder that communication and poor customer service is ranked as one of the biggest gripes.

Sadly, it doesn't stop there. When you put your property on the market, you're likely to receive a flurry of interest in the first few weeks. This is quite normal and your excited agent will be all too pleased to tell you about the new viewings that are coming in thick and fast. After this initial burst of activity things will go quiet and your agent will no longer be as forthcoming. That's because if they don't have any good news to tell you, many simply let customers suffer in silence.

In my experience, there's nothing worse than being kept in the dark. If interest has quietened down and there are no viewings, I find that customers like to know, because only by doing so, can we discuss how to stimulate interest. This might include considering new photographs, or different pricing strategy such as including some juicy buyer incentives.

Because I believe that the fragmented approach of the traditional estate agency model is not best suited to providing top-notch customer service, I work completely differently. I'll view your home myself, take down and prepare a fully detailed marketing description to sell. I'll personally take all of the photographs and then conduct the viewings.

This 'beginning-to-end' insight means that I know everything there is to know about the property. I'm able to speak in glowing terms about all of your home's best features. It enables me to overcome objections as they arise, but most importantly, as soon as a viewing has been conducted, I can feedback any comments and review them with my clients.

The feedback should always be given at the very least weekly but, beyond that, whenever the client requires it. In fact, all of my clients get my business card with my mobile number and can call me at any time. If I'm unavailable, I'll always call them back as soon as possible.

For me, one person should be accountable from beginning to end and that person should work alongside the client as their trusted guide. Given that other estate agents are fixed in their traditional ways, one may question why I persist with such an unorthodox approach? Quite simply it's because of the feedback my customers provide; the constant stream of amazing testimonials I receive, a sample of which I proudly display on my website. It works. They tell me time and time again that they value enormously the personal service that I provide them and that's why a lot of my business comes from word of mouth recommendations.

Did You Know?

According to an IPSOS MORI (Nov. 2018) poll, estate agents are the 5th most mistrusted profession. In the "Hall of Shame" they're only beaten by:

1. Advertising Executives
2. Politicians
3. Government Ministers
4. Journalists

Step 13

"WOW!!!"

Pitching Your House Price

From Step 11, you can find out how to get your house value/marketing appraisals by speaking to a number of estate agents. The time now comes to put your house on the market. You'll obviously take guidance from your chosen estate agent as to the right price to market your home, but in doing so you should make sure that you don't overvalue your property. If you do, you run the risk of taking it out of the reach of potential buyers.

Getting your house price right from the beginning is extremely important. That's because studies from the main portals suggest that in the first 14 days after your property has been listed, you're likely to receive twice the level of normal enquiries. Your honeymoon period is achieved because people looking for a house in your area will see it for the first time. Many potential buyers will have set up property alerts so that they get instant notifications of new listings. Lots of people browse online searching for properties, specifically looking for the most recent listings first. Referring back to Step 11, if you've fallen into the estate agency trap and overpriced your home (it's actually a breach of the consumer protection regulations 2008 to purposely overprice your property just to win your business.)

After a few weeks interest will wane and you'll have missed the maximum opportunity to sell. It's then very difficult to try and regain the lost momentum. If your property languishes on the market for a long time, it will no longer be found in 'recent listings' searches. Anybody who has seen it the first time around will simply skip past it. The only way to stimulate further interest will be to drop the price. This could mean that you end up with a final price lower than you would have otherwise achieved if it had been pitched correctly in the first place.

The consumer research company Which? found in their study that a house overvalued by just 5% took 64 days longer to sell and sold for £19,000 less, for an average value home, than homes marketed at a more representative price. This means that an agent who tries to win your business with a 'heady' valuation would end up costing you dearly.

That's why it's important to go with an agent that you can trust, rather than one that promises you a "too good to be true" marketing price that's impossible to achieve.

Another critical point you should take into consideration (and one that most estate agents are completely ignorant of) is making sure that you pitch your price to maximise your property's visibility on the property portals.

The common mistake by estate agents is to list a property just below a key price point, for instance marketing a house to sell at £199,950. The belief is that by keeping it below £200,000 it will appear more attractive to a buyer. Because, of course buyers are idiots and don't realise that £50 more makes £200,000! (Yep, estate agents really do believe this nonsense).

This concept is flawed. The portals list properties based upon the search criteria of the buyer. This is normally set to show the highest price properties first, but can be switched to show the lowest price first. Every Dumb and Dumber agent does the same thing. So, all you'll have succeeded in doing is finding yourself submerged in a sea of other listings, all at exactly the same price. You'll then re-surface somewhere several pages down the search results. But what this also means is that if you're smart and list your property at £200,000, you'll appear at the top of the search listing results.

Crucially, your listing will be in front of the masses of houses displayed at £199,950. However, it gets even better than that.

If you play around with Rightmove and Zoopla and take yourself through the process of searching for properties, you'll see that when you select the "price range" option, the list of price bands is shown initially with £10,000 increments. Beyond £300,000 the increments increase by larger amounts.

This is the journey that your potential buyer will take when searching for their home. So, if their budget is, say, £200,000 and their search is between £190,000 and £200,000, if you pitch your property at £200,000 yours will appear near the top. So wherever possible you should align your property's price with that of the price bandings used by the property portals.

But this also gives you a double bonus. By matching your property exactly to that of a price band, you'll not only appear in the searches of houses between say, £190,000 – £200,000, you'll also appear in the searches of houses between £200,000 – £210,000. In doing so you'll open yourself up to being seen by potentially twice as many people! This can, in turn, double your chances of getting viewers and selling your home.

Sadly, most agents don't have a clue about this technique, so you must make sure that your preferred estate agent is aware of it to give your home the best opportunity of selling. On the next page, I've listed the price bands used by Rightmove in May 2019. They do change from time to time, so it's important to check. Ideally, your house should be pitched exactly between one band and another to benefit from dual search listings. The prices shown in the table are exactly between two search bands.

Rightmove Price Search Bands:

£50,000	£220,000	£650,000
£60,000	£230,000	£700,000
£70,000	£240,000	£800,000
£80,000	£250,000	£900,000
£90,000	£260,000	£1,000,000
£100,000	£270,000	£1,250,000
£110,000	£280,000	£1,500,000
£120,000	£290,000	£1,750,000
£125,000	£300,000	£2,000,000
£130,000	£325,000	£2,500,000
£140,000	£350,000	£3,000,000
£150,000	£375,000	£4,000,000
£160,000	£400,000	£5,000,000
£170,000	£425,000	£7,500,000
£175,000	£450,000	£10,000,000
£180,000	£475,000	£15,000,000
£190,000	£500,000	£20,000,000
£200,000	£550,000	
£210,000	£600,000	

Zoopla's price bands are broadly similar with minor variations. Given that most people search Rightmove, simply stick to Rightmove's price bands when looking to list your house.

Remember that whilst pitching your house at one of these price points will help your property to appear in more search results, it's not a hard and fast rule.

If your house had a recommended marketing price of £750,000, you'd be caught between the bands at £700,000 and £800,000. To try and move to either band would not be in your best interests. Pitching at £700,000 may mean that you end up getting less than you would otherwise have achieved, and going for £800,000 is likely to put off buyer's due to overpricing.

So, whilst this technique works most of the time, there may be occasions when it's not right for you.

Top Tip!

Try to align your property price with the Rightmove/Zoopla price bands. You'll appear in twice as many search enquiries and double your exposure online as a result.

Tell your current agent straight away if they are doing it wrong!

Step 14

Using a Reputable Estate Agent

'Reputable' and 'Estate Agent' are not often words used in the same sentence! It can be difficult to find out whether or not you are using an estate agent with a poor reputation, but there are some useful hints and tips that can help you to minimise your risk.

One tip is to search online to see if there is any bad press or complaints showing up on forums. Another is to check the agent's professional affiliations.

Estate and letting agents currently do not need to be qualified to practice. There are bodies such as the National Association of Estate Agents (NAEA), the Association of Residential Letting Agents (ARLA), the National Approved Lettings Scheme (NALS) and Safe Agent which provide certification to confirm the qualifications of their members.

I'm a local Branch Director of EweMove Sales and Lettings Ltd. EweMove Sales and Lettings Ltd is a member of ARLA.

All estate agents have to comply with the Estate Agent Act 1979 and be registered with an approved Ombudsman scheme. These schemes provide a form of independent redress should a consumer have an unresolved complaint and seek to have a determination. In certain circumstances they can also award compensation.

Most complaints to the Ombudsman relate to failings in administration, although some sellers complain when they believe that offers on a property have not been put to them. It's for this reason that the Property Ombudsman Scheme sets out approved Codes of Practice that their members should adhere to.

For example, it stipulates that any offer made on a property should be put to a seller in every case within a reasonable period of time, normally deemed to be two working days. This should be in writing and the only exception to this is where the vendor has given specific instructions that any offer below a certain level will not be considered.

I'm a member of The Property Ombudsman Scheme. Details of the Ombudsman service can be found here:

www.tpos.co.uk

You can also use this site to search members and make sure that the estate agent that you're choosing is currently part of the ombudsman service.

Alternative ombudsman schemes include:

www.ombudsman-services.org
www.theprs.co.uk

A simple way of checking an estate agent's accreditations is to look for these approved regulative body logos:

The final tip to satisfy yourself about the credibility of an estate agent is to see if they've won any recent industry awards.

Everybody will say that they're the best, but do they have independent industry acknowledgement as proof?

Look for nationally recognised industry awards. There are over 20,000 sales and letting agents in the UK and national awards allow the cream to rise to the top.

So, a shameless plug…

Over the years EweMove have scooped awards for Innovation, Best Property Management, Best Newcomer, being the Best Estate Agent to Work For and The Best Estate Agency Franchise.

EweMove is the only national brand to win a top 3 prize in both sales and lettings at The EA Masters. We feature in the Best Estate Agents Guide 2019. This research was produced after extensive mystery shopping and analysis of statistics on Rightmove. This research was conducted by Rightmove and the Property Academy in 2018.

This award means EweMove is the 3rd Best Agent in the whole of the UK - WOW!

But shiny awards are one thing, the real deal is what customers experience, day in, day out. We've being privileged to have thousands of house sellers trust us to help them move on. **We're the UK's Most Trusted Estate Agent.**

We've had thousands of 5 star reviews and we're proud that our customers have enabled us to become the No.1 rated and most trusted estate agent in the UK on the independent consumer review website, Trustpilot (May, 2019)

Step 15

Property Portals

Most house hunters browse online now rather than visiting traditional high street branches, given this you can see the importance of getting fantastic photographs and floor plans together with a compelling description to use for your property brochure online.

The market is dominated by two main providers - Rightmove and Zoopla. Zoopla also own the trading brand Prime Location. To give you some idea of the power of these portals, Rightmove was the 23rd most visited website in the UK in 2018.

An independent review by Similar Web listed these portals as having the following visitor traffic during April 2019:

1.   Rightmove 59.1m (57%)
2.   Zoopla/Prime Location (ZPG) 32.3m (31%)
3.   On The Market (OTM) 12.4m (12%)

Those numbers are staggering! By listing on the major two (which EweMove does), the combined monthly visitor numbers are over 91 million!

Rightmove is currently the clear leader, but there are signs that Zoopla is beginning to catch up. So, why is this important?

Well, some agents only list their properties with one of the major portals in order to keep their costs down. This means that you'll lose out on a significant number of potential buyers who don't get to see your property's details. According to website auditor Nielsen, over 80% of the traffic on these sites is unduplicated. So, 4 out of 5 people simply use one portal exclusively as their preference.

The agents who do this are putting their own selfish interests (saving money on portal fees) ahead of their customers, who want the biggest and best exposure to buyers.

In order to give your property, the best chance of selling you need to make sure that it's listed on the two major portals.

I market on Rightmove and Zoopla, hitting 98% of buyers.

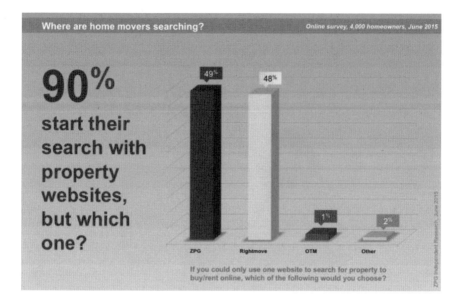

And this survey also found that 31% of buyers found their home exclusively on Zoopla. So, agents that cut corners and costs should be avoided if you want the best chance of selling.

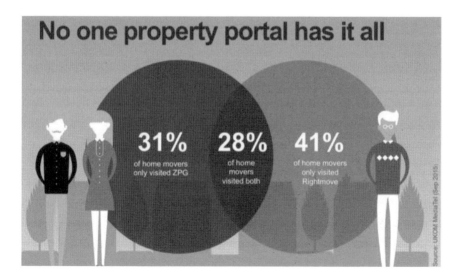

Step 16

Estate Agents Websites

Now you may be somewhat surprised at the notion that an estate agent's website is important when it comes to selling your home. But bear with me. You've seen from Step 15 the importance of property portals in view of the fact that most house hunters find their home online. When a buyer finds a property they are interested in, they then visit the estate agents own website…

Put in simple terms, how your home looks and how it's reflected to the wider world, will be directly impacted by its presentation on your estate agent's website!

If your estate agent has a boring, bland and poorly presented 'template' website (which sadly many have), that drab image could reflect very poorly on your property. So, before deciding which estate agent to use, you should take time out to review their website. Have a gander at their existing properties and make sure that they are presented professionally and in an appealing way.

Key things to look out for are:

1. The site should be simple to navigate
2. You should be able to find properties quickly
3. It should be clear and beautifully presented
4. Photographs should be immaculately set out
5. You should be able to download a professionally designed PDF brochure

Because we know the importance of our website as part of the buyer's journey, EweMove have invested tens of thousands of pounds and enlisted the help of professional designers to ensure that it looks amazing and is simple to use. This starts with a navigation bar that allows users to find a branch, properties or request a valuation estimate in one simple step.

We also know that people have a very poor impression of estate agents, perceiving them to be untrustworthy and boring (according to a IPSOS MORI survey, the 5th least trusted profession). For this reason, we try to engage users, like your potential buyer, by making our website fun and friendly so that they'll be more receptive to the properties that they're looking to view. What I find irritating is the fact that lots of agents prefer to spend vast sums of money on swanky offices with cappuccino making coffee machines. These do little other than serve to impress their friends. That's despite the hard evidence that hardly any buyers wander through their doors!

The website should also make it very easy for the potential buyer to contact the estate agent in order to enquire further or book a viewing. That's why our telephone number is shown at the top right of the screen, we're open 24 hours a day for calls and we allow customers to book their own viewings online if they wish to.

In fact, we picked up an award from the Times and Sunday Times for innovation in respect of the Ewereka system that powers our website engine.

The EweMove website has also won industry awards for being user friendly and engaging.

Top Tip!

Make sure that you look on your estate agent's website before instructing them. You need to make sure it's easy to navigate and the property listings look fantastic. Dull websites will make your property appear drab, dreary and unattractive.

Step 17

Opening Hours

This topic might be one that you would normally give little regard to, but hang in there.

Your ideal buyer is more than likely going to work during the day and have their free time during the evening and at weekends. This is the time during which they'll browse online looking for their perfect new home. This is also the time when the vast majority of estate agents have their doors slammed shut!

So, here's the problem. When your perfect buyer has spotted your property and excitedly jumped over to your estate agent's website to find out how to book themselves onto a viewing, they've got little option but to either submit an email enquiry or, alternatively leave a voice mail. The next day, depending upon the efficiency of staff in attendance, the agent will try and phone back the now, less than excited viewer. They're now busy at work and are unable to take the call. As time passes your potential buyer's interest is likely to fade. They'll also have the opportunity to explore other properties that may now take preference over yours. That's especially the case if the other agent that they call is able to secure them a quick viewing slot.

This in my opinion is a massive failing on the part of many agents who continue to run their businesses like cottage industries by failing to move with the times. We now live in a world where we demand supermarkets to be open 24 hours, home delivery and our insurance companies to be on hand when we're free to speak to them. Why don't estate agents provide the same level of customer service that consumers are increasingly beginning to expect?

As far back as 2012 we introduced 24 hour opening to enable us to receive calls from prospective viewers who could then be booked onto allocated viewing slots.

But interestingly, whilst we are available to speak to customers 24/7, we find that the vast majority prefer to interact with us online. When you think about it, it's really quite understandable. Who in their right mind would wish to speak to an estate agent if they could avoid it!

In order to take advantage of this, we allow prospective viewers to book their own viewing slots from the comfort of their own armchairs. They can even make offers to buy a property online. The vast majority of our viewings are now arranged in this way.

And the statistics bear testament to the success of this service. Over one third of our enquiries come outside of normal office hours. These potential buyers and additional viewings could well have been missed if the option had not been made available (as is the case with other high street agents).

Beyond this, when looking for an estate agent, you should make sure that they provide a flexible service for conducting viewings at both weekends and, if required in the evening. Ultimately, the customer is king and if your buyer wants to view at a particular time of the week, your estate agent should be accommodating to them. At the end of the day, contrary to what many agents like to believe, they're working for you, not for themselves.

Top Tip!

To make sure that you don't lose out on a potential buyer, choose an agent that has cover 24/7. 9-5 simply doesn't cut it in today's housing market.

Innovative Marketing

When it comes to doing your due diligence, you should check that your potential estate agent covers all of the basics. That is:

1. They're on all of the major portals such as Rightmove, Zoopla and Prime Location
2. They do 2D and stunning 3D floor plans
3. They're Professional Photography Academy trained
4. They've got an incredible website to showcase your home

Beyond this you need to explore how effective they are at marketing peoples' homes. The reason for this is that many old-fashioned agents simply rely upon outmoded methods to sell houses. That is, they'll stick a boring "For Sale" board outside your home (which is more about selling themselves, rather than your property) and if they're feeling particularly adventurous, they'll put an advert in the local rag.

Only 1% of buyers find their homes from the newspaper! Sadly, news print media is a dying form of marketing, along with their current readership. But estate agents still persist because it is a source of new instructions (rather than a good method to sell houses). They also don't know anything different.

This goes back to the problem of agents working in their own cottage industries. Good agents will adopt a far more radical approach. They'll have active and engaging social media sites, for example, Facebook and Twitter.

Facebook is particularly good and I use it to engage with local community groups and businesses. By fostering strong local relationships my site gets interest and followers. This then enables me to promote selective properties using social media to a wider audience. Of course, any estate agent engaging in social media should do so with a nicely presented Facebook and Twitter page. You can check out mine by following the links at the back of this book.

If they do carry out this method of marketing, you need to make sure that it's not boring and bland like every other agent in town. It needs to ooze personality. Given that the public perception of an estate agent is that of a faceless, unfriendly person, I try and break down these barriers by publishing my name and photo on all of my marketing material. By showing that I'm a nice person (well, both of my friends say that I am), they'll feel more inclined to speak to me for an informal chat.

This also filters through into my website. By making it light hearted, fun and engaging, it helps people to relax and feel at ease with the estate agency. By doing so, they're more likely to interact with me and feel more comfortable when getting in touch.

When it comes to property boards, your agent should seek to be innovative and help you to capture people's attention when they drive by. So many estate agency boards are boring and bland and fade into the background. You want the board to grab people's attention the instant that they pass by and let them know, in no uncertain terms, that your house is for sale.

That's why we spend considerable time planning and designing jaw dropping boards that quite literally stand out from the crowd.

A small number of people don't like them, but the vast majority love them. The key thing is - everybody remembers them! And that's the point. I'll do whatever it takes to make sure that my customers' properties get the attention that they deserve.

When you're looking to sell your home, you can get a feel for the marketing process of your potential agent by looking at the boards around your town, having a browse through their website and checking out their social media presence.

You'll get some shocking results, but hopefully you'll see some good examples of agents who are moving with the times and delivering the twenty first century marketing that their customers deserve.

Top Tip!

'For Sale' boards are a very important sales tool. Make sure that your agent has an eye-catching board that will really grab people's attention when they drive by.

What You Must Reveal

Beyond the features of your house and what's obviously apparent to your potential buyers when they come to view, there may be other aspects of your home and its surroundings, which may be of interest to your potential buyer. The question then is "What duty do you have to disclose things which may put off a potential buyer?".

Traditionally sellers have relied upon the maxim 'Caveat emptor', which is Latin for 'Let the buyer beware': i.e., it's not your obligation to disclose, but your buyer's responsibility to find out. This is no longer the case!

Protection for buyers and the duty to disclose any material information stems from the Consumer Protection from Unfair Trading Regulations 2008. Importantly, this makes the duty to disclose a joint one, applying to both the agent and the seller. As with any legislation, it's open to interpretation and it's currently a developing area of law with very few case precedents. The key question to ask yourself is "Do you know of any information relating to your property that might cause a buyer to make a different decision?" If you do, it must be disclosed.

There are certain things that do not require disclosure because they are readily apparent, for example the property's proximity to a nearby electricity pylon. Whilst it isn't necessary to set out the information within the marketing particulars, it should be given to a buyer at the earliest reasonable opportunity and before they put themselves to the trouble of attending a viewing.

Situations that may give rise to disclosure include:

* A murder or suicide at the property
* Previous flooding
* Previous subsidence
* Recent occupation by a convicted paedophile
* A neighbour dispute

Some of the above are clearly points of fact, but it's less straightforward when it comes to matters of opinion. For example, a neighbour playing loud music on the odd occasion might be one person's neighbour from hell, whereas someone else might not be bothered in the slightest. In my view, disputes will always require disclosure when any form of legal action has been taken, or where there's been intervention by a local authority or the police.

You should also bring to the viewer's/buyer's attention any problem previously identified on a survey from any earlier aborted sale. The reasoning for this is quite simple. If your subsequent would-be buyer goes ahead with a purchase and the self-same problem is highlighted, putting them to unnecessary expense, this could and should have been avoided.

One infamous case concerning a sale in the USA, was that of Stambovsky –v- Ackley. Here the Supreme Court found that a buyer could cancel and overturn their purchase of a property and claim for damages, because the seller had not warned them that the house was haunted! Previously the property featured in ghost tours and the resident poltergeists were local celebrities.

In the UK, the sales process goes a long way to ensure that any legal disputes are kept to a minimum. When you sell your property, you will have to complete a standard format 'Seller's Property Information' form. This sets out in great detail every aspect of your house. It includes; what you intend to leave, take with you and whether there have been any historic boundary disputes etc. But don't simply rely on this form as your safety net. If you believe there's something material to your buyer's decision, advise your estate agent and if necessary your conveyancing lawyer, just to be on the safe side.

To give you a good recent example of how this can apply, I know a buyer who was looking at a property and proceeded to contact the agent to arrange a viewing. A previous sale had fallen through when the former buyer had found out that a nearby chicken farm had resulted in neighbour protests following foul smells. The agent rightly pointed this out to the viewer and they took their own view that it wasn't a problem. He went on to purchase the property. By making sure that they had not fallen 'fowl' (I couldn't resist!) of their obligations to disclose, the agent had covered themselves and the seller.

Top Tip!

If you can think of anything that might put off a buyer from buying your house, let your estate agent and/or conveyancer know to cover your back. It's better to be safe than sorry.

Step 20

Sale Contracts

When your superstar estate agent has turned up in their shiny suit and brand-new tie and they've bowled you over with their winning pitch, they'll proudly produce their sales contract. They'll talk about the key facts, like the price that they hope to get you for your home and most people will then focus on the sales commission fee.

But what the vast majority of people fail to do is review and understand the terms of the contract, contained in the small print, usually on the reverse. This section will tell you all you need to know, including the little traps you need to watch out for to protect yourself.

In order to give you forewarning of the typical estate agency contract (but a nice one!), you can see an example of the model agreement that I use in Appendix 1. I've set out below the key parts to the vast majority of estate agency contracts that you'll come across.

1. Contract Length

The agreement will set out an Agency Term, or exclusive contract period. This is the minimum length of time that you are signed up and obligated to use the estate agent for. So, for example, if the estate agent says that the contract is for 12 weeks, you're tied into that agent for that period of time, even if they do a lousy job and you want to move elsewhere.

Estate agents use this lock-in period to give them sufficient time to sell the house. Referring back to Step 11, this period can be used by unscrupulous agents to give them breathing space when they know they've overvalued a property and cannot deliver on their promises. Indeed, some agents have teams that work on vendors in a bid to get them to reduce their prices to secure a sale before the clock runs out.

What you need to look out for is making sure that the Agency Term is not too long. 8 weeks is quite typical, 12 weeks+ in my opinion is far too long. You have to question why an estate agent would need this long, if they're as good as they say they are when they signed you up?

A long Agency Term for me is a red warning flag and it's not something that you should agree to. In my experience, long Agency Term time periods tend to be used more by online only estate agents, or an underperforming local agent.

Happy Sale Guarantee.

I've found that the fear of signing up with the wrong agent is one of the biggest concerns of house sellers. No one wants to be handcuffed by a poorly performing agent who has to rely on sneaky small print to keep you hostage against your will.

That's why we introduced our **"Happy Sale Guarantee"**.

In simple terms, if you're not 100% delighted with any aspect of my service, for any reason whatsoever, my unique, no quibble guarantee means that you can simply change your mind at any time and walk away, with nothing to pay at all. So, you enjoy the peace of mind knowing that you'll have the benefit of;

1. **No Minimum Contract Term**
   You can cancel at any time, so there's no risk

2. **No Cancellation Fee**
   If you do cancel before I find you a buyer, you won't have to pay me a penny

3. **No Sale – No Fee**
   No upfront, or pay later exit fees. You only pay me when the sale completes

2. Additional Charges

Beyond the standard fee for selling your home (which will either be a fixed amount, or a percentage commission based upon the sales price), the agent may offer to provide you additional marketing services. This could, for example, be to prepare professional brochures (see Step 10), or a professional video/aerial photographs.

The key point here is that any additional charges applied must be agreed by you and set out in writing. I make sure that any additional charges that do apply are written on the front of my contract and then signed off by the customer to make sure that they've been made perfectly clear (See Appendix 1).

Extra Services

It is standard within the industry for the estate agent to provide a range of additional services to your prospective buyer. These can include arranging a mortgage, insurance, recommending removal companies, conveyancing firms and surveyors. It's also common practice for the estate agent to receive a commission for such referrals directly from the third-party providers.

What you need to make sure doesn't happen, is the practice of your agent making the buyer's offer conditional upon them using the agent's own in-house recommended providers. For example, some agents have been known to suggest that buyers cannot even view your property, or make an offer, unless they use their in-house mortgage provider. This is not acceptable practice and it will put off many potential buyers. This in turn reduces your prospects of achieving a successful sale, because your home is no longer being made available to the widest possible audience.

3. Marketing Your Property

Your estate agent will recommend, quite rightly, that you have a 'For Sale' board outside your home. They need to obtain your consent before they can put one up.

Some people prefer not to have boards outside their home because they want to keep their activities secret from their neighbours. Given that we live in an online world, you'll soon find that your neighbours know all about your property listing. Indeed, their tongues are more likely to start wagging wondering why there's no board outside! So, this is more likely to lead to suspicion where none should even exist.

If you want to sell your home, then a 'For Sale' board is one of the great ways to market your home. Not least because it allows your potential buyers to find it when they're coming for a viewing. You should also remember that your neighbours are likely to know friends and acquaintances that may wish to move into the area. They could become your allies and the best source of your ultimate buyer.

I would therefore always recommend that you allow a marketing board to be placed outside your home when the time comes to sell.

4. Accessing the Property

Your estate agent should always arrange viewing appointments with you and where necessary make sure that you are in attendance, or that they carry out the accompanied viewing. They should not allow anybody to carry out a viewing of the property unaccompanied without your specific instruction.

This is for obvious reasons, such as protecting your home from theft or any other criminal activity. The best agents carry out accompanied viewings as standard.

Indeed I make this part and parcel of my service offering. The reason is quite simple. Evidence has shown that you are almost twice as likely to receive an offer from a viewer following an accompanied viewing. A viewing where the estate agent walks you around and tells you all about the property, not just an agent who holds the key.

The reasoning behind this is that when buyers are looking at a home, they tend to feel uncomfortable when the owners are present. Owners can also talk about features of the home that are of no interest to a potential buyer and in turn, put them off. A viewer might want to put forward an offer below the asking price, but feel awkward in front of the owner for fear of offending them.

A good estate agent, acting as a go-between for the parties, can take instructions from a buyer, relay this back to the seller and then negotiate to and fro between the parties. Ultimately the goal is to reach an acceptable solution without bringing any emotion or irrational behaviour into the proceedings.

You should always insist when you're looking for an agent to market your home, that you have one who provides accompanied viewings, by someone who knows your home inside and out, as standard.

5. Offers

Under the Codes of Practice set out for estate agents, they're duty bound to ensure that, prior to exchange of contracts, all offers at any time and for any amount are put forward to the seller for their consideration.

This even applies if the estate agent genuinely believes that the offer is ridiculous and will never be accepted. The only exception to this is if the agent has received specific instructions from the seller not to put forward offers below a certain amount or type – for example from a buyer who wants to offer an amount below which a seller has said that they will not even consider.

This obligation arises from historic complaints against estate agents for allegedly failing to put forward offers for fear of upsetting the apple cart on a proceeding sale. The suggestion was that estate agents were more concerned about securing an immediate commission, rather than the achieving the best price for their client. Agents must now keep a computer record of all offers put forward and, as a seller, you're entitled to request a copy.

Any offer received should be put forward to a seller as soon as reasonably possible. This is generally accepted to be no longer than two working days.

6. Type of Estate Agency Agreement

There are three main types of estate agency contract:

1.   Sole selling rights
2.   Joint agency
3.   Multiple agency

For further details as to how these sale arrangements work, read Step 21 – 'Estate Agency Sales Agreements'

7. Agreement Termination

As stated earlier in this Step, the Agency Term will run for a minimum period of normally between 12 weeks – 6 months. After this time the contract will continue, but will provide for a method of cancellation. This is normally in the form of either the seller or the agent serving notice upon the other of their intention to cancel. My agreement provides for a short 14-day notice period.

8. Energy Performance Certificate (EPC)

Before you can market your property, you or your estate agent must commission an EPC. This must be obtained no later than 7 days after the property has been marketed. For further details, read Step 35 – 'Energy Performance Certificates'.

9. Personal Interest

Your agent is duty bound to tell you whether or not they have a personal interest in any matters concerning the sale of your property. So, if a buyer puts forward an offer and that person has any association with the agent, for example an employee, associate, friend or family member, they have a duty to inform you of this.

The reason stems from historic complaints against estate agents for putting forward offers and recommendations from known associates. Sellers were aggrieved when they subsequently found out the buyer's relationship to the agent and believed that they'd been short changed. The complaints centred on potential conflicts of interest when the seller felt that they should have achieved a better sale price. In some cases, this resulted in legal claims for compensation.

Estate agents must be seen to be whiter than white and if an offer comes forward flagged as being from a 'Personal Interest' buyer, you can fully consider the circumstances behind it, form your own opinion as to whether or not it's acceptable and then make an informed decision as a result.

Unoccupied Properties

If you're selling a property and have moved out, you need to be aware that the estate agent's contract will include a disclaimer stating that you're responsible for the repair and mains services in order to protect your property until it's sold. Good precautions to take include turning off the water and draining down the central heating system to avoid burst pipes during winter. Turning off the gas supply to central heating and other installations helps avoid fire and explosion risks. You should also inform your insurance company that the property is unoccupied to check that you're adequately covered.

Many insurers have exclusion clauses, which state that cover does not extend beyond (typically) 30 days after the date from which the property was last occupied. But by giving your insurer notice, they can adjust your policy and premium accordingly and make sure that you are protected. Sadly, many customers don't realise this until it comes to making a claim, by which time, it's too late.

Whilst the property is empty you continue to be liable for your services such as gas, electricity and council tax. It's wise to put in place a redirection of your mail immediately to your new address and also to check on the property every 7 – 14 days. You may wish to tend to the gardens, particularly in summer months.

The Property Ombudsman

Every estate agent is obliged to be a member of an ombudsman redress scheme. This allows you to lodge a complaint if you are unhappy with the service. This will initially be dealt with in-house.

If you remain unsatisfied, the complaint can be referred to the independent ombudsman for review. They will make an adjudication and can, if appropriate, make an award of compensation. I am a member of The Property Ombudsman Scheme (TPOS), details of which can be found at www.tpos. co.uk

You can check out whether or not your agent is a member by searching online at this site, or looking for this logo:

10. Cooling Off Period

Under the provisions of the Consumer Contract (Information, Cancellation and Additional Charges) Regulations 2013, where an estate agent signs up a client in their own home, i.e. not in the estate agency offices, that customer is entitled to a 14 day right to cancel.

You should note that this cooling off period does not apply if you sign up to the terms at the agent's office.

An agent must include a written notice of how to exercise the right to cancel as part of their standard terms and conditions. Mine can be seen in Appendix 1.

Top Tip!

Most agents promise that they can sell your house quickly, but then tie you into a long-term contract. If they are as good as they say they are, you must question why? Demand a contract with no minimum term and a 14-day cancellation clause. This is included in my 'Happy Sale Guarantee'.

Step 21

'We'll take care of you'

Estate Agency Sales Agreement

There are three main types of estate agency contract, all of which have their upsides and downsides. I'll explain each of them in turn and tell you how they work in practice. You can also see my standard wording for the various types within my Terms and Conditions in Appendix 1.

1. Sole Selling Rights

One of the most common forms of Sale agreement. It means that you're giving permission to your agent to sell your home, to the exclusion of all other agents, within the minimum contract period.

It also means that you have to pay the estate agent even if you find the buyer. That's because the agent will make the point that the buyer would not have known about the property being on the market for sale, but for their marketing activities. It also removes potential conflicts as to whether or not the seller is being open and honest in terms of where the buyer actually came from.

Agreements normally include a provision that if the buyer was introduced by the agent during the initial agency minimum term, but then the contract is ended and at some time in the future the buyer goes on to purchase the property, then the agent will also be paid. This is to protect the estate agent from a seller cancelling a contract to avoid paying a fee, but then going on to sell the property to the buyer.

The benefit of the Sole Selling Rights agreement is that because you're committed to one agent, the agent knows that they'll be paid if they go on to sell your home. This should incentivise them to do their utmost to sell your property.

The downside is that if you instruct a poor agent, you're stuck with them during the minimum contract period. Whereas if you instruct on a joint or multi-agency contract and have another agent working on your behalf, you would hope that at least one of them will do a good job.

2. Joint Agency Agreements

This is where you instruct a number of estate agents. Normally it will be two. In this instance, you have to pay one fee that's split between the estate agents once a sale is agreed, irrespective of which estate agent secures the sale.

Again, it's likely to include a provision that the fee will be payable after the agreement has ended, if you ultimately sell to a buyer introduced by one of the agents during the original contract period.

The joint agents will agree between themselves how the fee charged will be split. It's often the case that the agent who secures the sale gets the lion's share of the spoils. Typically divided on a two thirds/one third basis.

The advantage of this type of instruction is that you'll have more than one agent working for you and hopefully one of them will do a better job.

The disadvantage is that both agents may feel disincentivised and hope that the other agent does all of the hard work allowing them to benefit from doing relatively little. Ultimately, you'll end up paying a much larger fee.

3. Multiple Agency

This works in a similar way to a Joint Agency. You instruct a number of agents, normally two. Here it's a case of 'Winner takes all'. The agent that finds you the buyer receives the full sales commission fee.

This can be a good way of generating competition between agents, but the downside is that estate agents don't like working on this basis. That's because they feel demotivated if they're doing lots of work and end up getting nothing. You'll also find that the fee that you'll pay is likely to be significantly higher than if you instructed an agent on a Sole Selling Rights basis.

Which One is the Most Suitable?

I'm able to provide any form of contract to my clients, dependent upon the particular circumstances of their house and what's appropriate to help them to get a sale.

I believe that in the majority of instances, a Sole Selling Rights contract works best. The fee is kept at a competitive level and the agent is only paid if they achieve a successful result.

Multi-Agency and Joint Agency agreements are more appropriate for certain types of market, such as areas of London where it's extremely competitive. They're also a good idea where a house will benefit from a two-pronged marketing strategy with different types of estate agent. For example, higher value large estate homes may benefit by being marketed within the traditional local town, but also showcased with a prestige agent across a wider regional area. That's because extremely expensive executive homes are in limited supply. The type of occupant that seeks these houses is quite often prepared to travel to find the right one.

When instructing an agent, you need to make sure that you're not exposing yourself to paying dual fees. For example, if you instruct an agent on a Sole Selling Rights basis and you've not yet run the course of your initial minimum contract term, you're still liable to pay that agent's fee. This might arise if you're unhappy with the first agent's service and then decide to instruct a new agent.

That's why it's important to make sure that the Agency Term (or minimum contract), is not excessively long i.e. it should be no longer than 12 weeks. I'd certainly view 6 months or more as being totally excessive.

Finally, you should be aware that your liability to pay the estate agent's fee normally applies when exchange of contracts takes place. That's when you've signed your legal paperwork to confirm the sale with your solicitors. Normally payment is delayed and the commission is deducted from your sale proceeds by your solicitor when the sale goes through.

The only other issue that you need to be made aware of is that in most Sole Selling Rights agreements, you're also liable to pay a fee if the estate agent finds a "Ready, willing and able buyer" if you pull out of the sale at the last minute. The rationale for this is that the agent has done their job and found a buyer who is willing to put forward an acceptable offer to you. If you then change your mind, it would be unfair if, through no fault of the agent, they don't get paid for all the work that they've done.

Step 22

Fixed Fee or Commission Only

The traditional way in which estate agents have sold homes is to charge a percentage of the sales price as a commission, plus the current rate of VAT. So, if you sell your house for £200,000 with a 1.5% commission, you'll pay £3,000 plus VAT. If the VAT rate was 20%, the total amount payable would be £3,600. Be careful, because all agents should quote their fees inclusive of VAT, but sadly many still don't.

Estate agents would argue that this is fair because if they get a lower price, their fee will be reduced accordingly. Similarly, if they work hard to get the best price, they'll get slightly more. This in my view is not a strong argument given the relatively small amounts involved as a percentage of the asking price. So, a £1,000 increase in a sale price will only earn the agent £15. It's hardly a strong incentive to squeeze every last penny from a buyer.

Consumer groups quite rightly make the point that using a percentage rate does not allow the customer to clearly see what they're actually paying. Trying to work out what a 1.75% fee translates to, from an unknown final sale price, is very difficult.

Against this backdrop the recommended consumer guidelines now state that fees should be clearly set out and when percentages are used, an example of what that will potentially translate to should be given. This will be derived from the recommended marketing price and must clearly include the VAT element and total.

That's why on my agreements the front page clearly states an estimate of the fee payable, including VAT, so that the seller is not left to second guess. They can also see how this charge compares to the competition, assuming of course that the competition is as equally transparent! Unfortunately, a lot of estate agents are stuck in the past and simply promote percentages, without referring to VAT and without clearly setting out what this means in black and white.

The next thing to consider is whether you want to pay a fixed upfront fee, or one based upon a successful sale. A fee payable on sale is the traditional way of working. Paying upfront is a relatively new concept and is often promoted by 'online only' estate agents (see Step 23).

As with everything, there are two sides to the coin. Here are my views on the pros and cons of paying fixed fees upfront:

Fixed Fee Model

Pros	Cons
You know exactly what you are paying for up front Often far cheaper than paying based upon achieving successful sale	A lot of houses do not end up selling (up to 50%), so you end up paying out and losing your money Having paid the fee, you're trapped with that agent and are unlikely to want to move having already shelled out Once the agent has the fee, there is no incentive for them to work hard to get the sale Some agents promote 'No Upfront Fees' – They'll still charge you later when it hasn't sold If you change your mind and no longer want to sell, you've lost your money Some people question whether an online agent can provide a great service, by charging so little

The online only estate agents, or the small number of high street agents who offer an upfront fixed fee service, will point out the benefits and disadvantages of the traditional commission based model. These can be summarised as follows:

Commission Only Model

Pros	Cons
It is a low risk option.	Commission only, based upon a successful sale is generally more expensive than an upfront fixed fee
If the seller changes their mind and removes the property from the market, they haven't lost any money	
The agent is only paid on success	
The agent is hungrier and incentivised to do a good job until the sale completes	
If the estate agent does a bad job the seller can switch to a new agent, without losing any money	
A large percentage of houses don't sell, saving the client from losing money	

At the end of the day, whether or not somebody chooses to go for a fixed fee, or percentage commission, largely depends upon the seller's profile. I find that sellers who are price sensitive, rather than service led, tend to go with the low cost cheaper option.

In doing so they are confident that the house will sell and assume that all agents are generally the same in terms of their service offering. Problems arise when the house doesn't sell, or they receive poor service/lack of any back-end feedback.

The Property Academy Survey of 2017 reports that 78% of people chose an agent based upon the one that they liked and trusted.

In my view, the best price for your home is best achieved by using a commission only agent. At the end of the day, if the agent has done a bad job, the client might be upset, but they can move on to a new agent and not feel bitter. That's because they've not lost out financially.

Step 23

Online or Local Agent

Times have moved on, most house hunters browse online in the evening, or at weekends rather than visiting traditional branches.

Given that the most house hunters are searching on major property portals you could well take the view that there's no need to use a traditional high street agent.

In view of the fact that online agents can give you access to the main property portals, such as Rightmove and Zoopla, you may want to explore whether or not online agents can provide you with a cheaper alternative.

Against this backdrop, it's interesting to look at what is actually happening in the marketplace. Rightmove, said in January 2017 that online agents only had just over 6% share of new listings. As ever, whether or not to list with an online only agent, or use a local agent, is subject to arguments both for and against.

The facts show that around 40% of online agent's properties don't sell (TwentyEA, 2019). It's like playing online roulette with your house and hoping to land on red.

If you get black, not only have you lost all of your money, but also, you've suffered the frustration of having placed your life on hold for many months until you eventually bite the bullet and change agents.

I've set out my own views in the following table:

Pros	Cons
They can normally provide access to all of the major portals including Rightmove, Zoopla and Prime Location	About 40% of houses do not end up selling according to Twenty EA data.
Generally, far cheaper than a traditional estate agent	When no fixed fee is charged upfront, the minimum Agency Term period can be longer
It's attractive to people who believe that the initial price is more important than service and final sales price	Providers can be hundreds of miles from your home, unable to understand your local market, or meet potential buyers
It appeals to people who like to take risks and gamble in the hope of saving money	Customers choose an agent based upon a person they instinctively trust and like. This comes from having a face to face meeting
	An online agent is less likely to be able to provide accompanied viewings
	An online agent will be less able to address buyer enquiries such as the benefits of the local area, commuter links and amenities

As with most things, it generally boils down to a matter of price. You can undoubtedly make savings in terms of the commission by using an online agent, but in my opinion, this often comes at the cost of service. In my experience, people prefer to meet a local person, who knows the area, the housing market, local parks etc.

Someone they can relate to and who will have things in common with your potential buyers, which helps to put them at ease. This builds rapport and provides a means of instant communication with the seller to help them move forward with the property sale.

Whilst my view is admittedly going to be biased, I believe that the small additional price that you pay by using a traditional local agent is more than outweighed by the potential to get a higher price for your property upon sale.

This comes from being able to provide a better market appraisal service, a better means of negotiating with the buyer and ultimately securing the highest possible sale price.

So, whilst consumers may believe that they are saving money by using an online agent, they may lose thousands of pounds by not getting the best price for their house. This could mean that they end up losing out in the long run. Whilst these are my own views, I'm pleased to say that they are supported by research from clients that have recently used estate agents and reported their feedback.

The Property Academy Home Moving Trends Survey of 2017 found that only 19% of people chose an agent based upon them having the cheapest fee. The findings showed that when it came down to the final choice of which agent to use, 72% said, "The agent had a good reputation".

This represents the fact that people still like local, so agents need to offer a great brand locally and great service and then people will choose them.

Step 24

Premium Listings

Your estate agent may offer you an enhanced service by way of a Premium listing. These are provided by both Rightmove and Zoopla and they both work in a similar way. During this step, I'll explain how they work on Rightmove.

When your property is listed on the online property portals, they'll appear with a standard thumbnail picture and a small summary description, normally limited to 300 characters. So how can you make your property stand out?

With a Premium Listing, the default setting is to have an enhanced display, with one large main picture and three additional thumbnail pictures. Rightmove promotes this with a larger display, making it stand out against the backdrop of standard sized listings.

You'll also have a callout banner on the bottom right that is set by default to say 'Premium Listing'. A lot of agents don't change this, but Rightmove gives a range of alternatives including:

- Stamp duty paid
- Generous garden
- Open to offers
- Recently renovated
- Attention investors
- Stunning views

There are 96 options to choose from. If you do opt for a Premium Listing, to make sure that you give your property the best chance of standing out, choose one that's going to show off your home's best features and appeal to your potential purchaser.

An example of how a premium listing will look on Rightmove:

Fewer agents upgrade their properties to Premium on Zoopla and smart agents use this fact to their advantage. Your property has more chance of standing out from the crowd.

Here's how a Zoopla Premium listing looks:

£375,000 Guide price

🛏4 🛁3 🛋2

4 bed semi-detached house for sale

Condor Drive, Leighton Buzzard LU7

Time For Tea!... Sit back, relax and enjoy the views and walks over Astral Lake Park in this nearly new, showhome condition, 4 Bedroom home... This home has been road tested but barely warmed up the tyres so come and take the wheel and drive on to ...

🚊 Leighton Buzzard (1.6 miles) 🚊 Cheddington (3.2 miles)

📷 13

✓ Garage

✓ En Suite

Listed on 7th Feb 2019 by
EweMove Sales & Lettings -
Leighton Buzzard, LU7

📞 01525 204836 **   ✉ Contact   ★ Save   ⊘ Hide

Advantages of Premium Listings

Rightmove's Premium Listings attract more buyer enquiries. That's people looking, clicking and viewing the property in more detail. This will translate into more viewers, offers and a quicker sale.

If you want the very best chance of selling you should upgrade to Premium on both portals. You're now almost doubling the amount of interest from buyers.

The Cost

When it comes to paying for the service, Rightmove and Zoopla recommend that agents should charge £250 each for a Premium Listing. The question is, is it worth it?

Well, the first thing I'd say is; don't pay the full £500! Agents will probably be paying less than this amount to Rightmove and Zoopla for the privilege, so you can negotiate. Or you can ask for it be included as part of the sales commission package.

Of course, your house might sell straight away. So, by not getting an enhanced listing, you could save yourself a few quid. But are you saving money?

Because if you expose yourself to lots more buyers, you're more likely to create bidding competition which will help you to get a far better price.

My firm view is that clients are always best served by going for a Premium Listing. Let me explain why.

Surveys from Rightmove show that a property gets the most interest during the first 14 days. This is because it's new to the market; people have set up their property alerts on houses that interest them in a particular area and lots of people search for the most recent listings first.

If this is the most opportune moment and you're going to get double the normal level of exposure, it makes sense to get an additional boost.

By having a Premium Listing on both Zoopla and Rightmove, you'll benefit by increasing the number of interested enquiries. This should translate into you getting almost double the level of interest. This leads to a better chance of a higher price and a quicker sale. Given the costs of selling a house, the small additional price for a Premium Listing is, in my opinion, a complete 'no-brainer'.

Step 25

The First 14 Days

When you've chosen your estate agent and the property goes live, there's a flurry of activity and emotion. Both excitement about taking the first step on your new journey and fear as to what lies ahead. Will other people fall in love with your home just as you have done?

Almost instantly you're likely to get interest from potential buyers. This means that there's no time to get your house ready for viewings, carry out repairs, do the tidying up of the garden and all of those other little jobs that you've put off for another day. That's why it's crucial that before you market your home and present it to the world, you've carried out Steps 2 – 5. You want to make sure that your home is in perfect condition to do itself justice.

Evidence from the property portals such as Rightmove and Zoopla point to properties receiving double the level of interest in the first 14 days. That's because your would be buyers will be scouring the market for new opportunities and have alerts set up to bring the latest listings to their attention.

Against this backdrop of enhanced exposure, you need to do everything you can to ride the wave. That's why I always recommend boosting the level of interest during this honeymoon period by opting for a Premium Listing (see Step 24).

During this time, a great tip is to offer would be buyers the option to view your property at an open viewing. This is on an advertised date and time where anybody who has an interest in the property can simply drop by at the allocated time and view your home.

Open viewings work well for a number of reasons:

1. Your potential buyer doesn't need to make an appointment, so they're not going to be put off by having to call an estate agent

2. I recommend that you stage the viewing at a weekend, which is the most convenient time for most buyers

3. A potential buyer who initially may only have a lukewarm interest, can become stirred up into a hot prospect because they've been easily able to attend an open viewing

4. Lots of people in attendance together creates a buzz of excitement

5. When would-be buyers see other people interested, they'll become worried that they might lose out. This encourages them to take action quickly rather than remaining firmly sat on the fence

6. Buyers are more willing to attend an open viewing because, as part of a group, they feel less pressured

If your property has been on the market for a number of months, viewers are more likely to come around to view your home on a one-to-one basis. So, you'll be unable to get a large number of people together and gain all of the benefits that come with having an open viewing. That's why I strongly recommend them as part of your initial 14-day sales plan.

Another benefit is that in a short period of time you may well receive an offer on your property. If a number of people submit offers at the same time, a good estate agent will be able to negotiate between them in order to secure you the best possible price.

A word of caution. During this initial flurry of activity, with hopefully offers coming in, you need to keep a sense of perspective. You can get lulled into a false sense of security believing that your house will easily sell and that the interest that you've enjoyed on day one is 'normal' and will simply continue...

You need to stay objective and remember that this initial period is your property's peak selling time. You should not get overly greedy or unrealistic in terms of the offers being put forward. Here you need to take advice from your estate agent as to whether or not they believe the offer is realistic in the context of the prevailing market and any recent comparable sales nearby.

There have been countless examples of sellers confidently dismissing offers during the first 14 days in the firm belief that in the next few weeks, a higher offer is bound to materialise. Once they come to the dawning realisation that interest in the property slows over time, they may look back and regret their decision. They might try to desperately reignite previous interest, only to find that the buyer has moved on. Obviously, there's a fine balance between waiting to get the best offer and being unrealistic which may ultimately result in you missing the boat. That's why you need to get good advice from an agent who has been through this process many times before. They can guide you as to the suitability of any offer.

Because the first 14 days is going to be your best time to sell, it's also when you must do your utmost to present your property in its best light. So, you should go the extra mile by getting new colour coordinated toiletries, bathroom accessories, fresh flowers, fresh fruit and lovely scented candles and tea lights etc. And if you've followed all of these steps successfully, hopefully you'll get a fantastic offer for your property. Then you can start planning your next move into your new dream home…

Step 26

Weekly Feedback

I've already covered off in Step 25 that during the first 14-days, you'll experience a burst of activity and you should hopefully be delighted with your estate agent's service. Indeed, because of the number of viewings and potential offers that may be being generated, your agent is likely to be in regular contact with you, sharing all of the good news stories.

If your house doesn't sell quickly, as the weeks and months pass, it's important that the estate agent stays in regular contact with you. This should be at least weekly, giving you feedback, updates and advice on how to move your property forward.

One of the biggest areas of complaint from customers in respect of estate agents is the lack of communication, particularly if there's no good news. Sellers who find that the property is no longer receiving any interest will quickly become despondent if they feel that their agent has abandoned them when they no longer hear from them. My view is that when a house has not sold initially, this is where the good estate agents really earn their money! Any half decent agent can sell a house in a buoyant market, but it's only the really good ones that can go the extra mile and still help to sell houses when the going gets tough.

You also need to bear in mind that houses will not always sell straight away and that the average time will vary considerably for different parts of the country.

Hometrack data from 2018 showed that the average time to sell in the UK was 10.4 weeks. The best region being Scotland at 5.8 weeks, with the region being the north-east at 13.8 weeks.

You also need to remember that after securing a sale, it normally takes around three months for the sale to complete. That's because all sides have to arrange their moves and go through the conveyancing process.

So, whilst you should not be concerned or unduly alarmed if interest starts to slow down, it's still vitally important that you get ongoing and regular feedback from your estate agent at all times. This is particularly to allow you to review the market and then consider what additional steps you may wish to take in order to secure a sale.

One of the most important parts of an agent's role is to give you the viewer feedback. That's why I believe that it's vital to carry out accompanied viewings (See Step 28). The problem with many estate agents is that they expect the vendor to do the viewings. Or alternatively, they'll send a random person from the office. So, you end up with no consistent feedback. Worse still, lots of agents allow the office junior/administrator to chase-up feedback in an ad-hoc manner. Once a potential buyer has left the property and decided that it's not for them, they've got no interest in going out of their way to provide feedback. So, you've lost out on a brilliant opportunity to understand your property through the eyes of your viewers. By carrying out accompanied viewings you get the benefit of instant feedback from every viewing.

Many agents worry about giving negative feedback or telling their client bad news. Clients want to hear it and need the truth, because ultimately, they can then do something about it.

Another part of the estate agent's role is to give you feedback on how your property is performing on the portals such as Rightmove. Remember, these portals are going to be your key selling tool in finding a buyer, because most house hunters find their home online. If your property is performing poorly, then you're going to be at a significant disadvantage.

These portals allow member estate agents to provide Client Property Performance reports. This enables you to see how your property is performing. An example report is shown below:

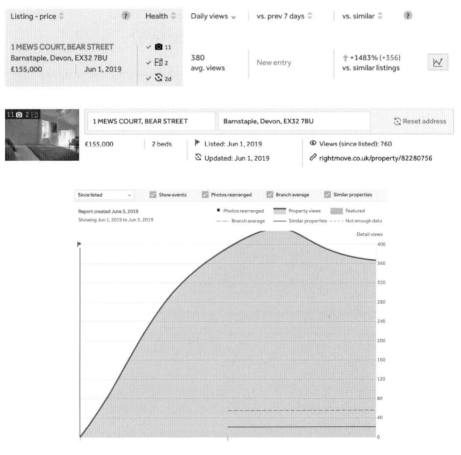

The data gives you three statistics as follows:

1. The number of times your property has been clicked on to see more details

After appearing in the initial summary search listings (above), this tells you how many times somebody has clicked through to read your property details in full. This is the most important data because it shows you how much interest your property is generating. Generally speaking, the more people who click through and read your full listing details, the more likely you are to get viewers to make appointments.

Rightmove work out an average no. of the daily views. They also display the stats within a graph format which is useful to understand how your property performance increases and decreases over time.

2. Health of your property listing

To ensure your listing performs highly on Rightmove, it's got to pass certain health checks. You can see on the left this property has 11 photographs, 2 floor plans, a 2D and a 3D plot plan and has been refreshed within 2 days which Rightmove validates as good numbers.

It's important that your agent refreshes your listing to stop it sticking. A simple change of photograph order can make a big difference.

3. VS. similar

This compares the property to similar properties on Rightmove at the moment. 1483% is a huge improvement compared to the other 356 properties available. This stat is higher due to the listing been relatively new as well as having professional quality photographs and a healthy number of floor plans!

The importance of these reports is that they give you an empirical measure of how your property is performing. If the number of clicks is poor, between you and your agent you need to discuss and review what can be done to improve them.

There are three main reasons why a house might not be stimulating interest:

1. The house itself! If it's in poor condition and poorly presented for the price, it will obviously have difficulty selling

2. Marketing: If the property is not marketed across all the main channels, you'll have less interest. If it's on all the main portals, such as Rightmove, Zoopla and Prime Location, it has fantastic photographs, it has 2D and 3D floor plans, plot plans, in conjunction with a fantastic description, you've got everything you need in terms of your marketing (which of course I provide as standard!)

3. The price: If the house is in fantastic condition and the marketing is all in order, ultimately the only thing that can stimulate interest is adjusting the price. At the end of the day, the market is the only true, impartial judge of what your house is really worth. That's why you always need to listen to the market feedback (viewer interest) and the portal click through rate reports. You can then understand whether or not the property has been pitched at the right price. That's why Step 11 – 'Getting Your Market Appraisal' and Step 13 – 'Pitching Your House Price', are so important

When discussing why a property has not sold, your estate agent needs to be open and honest with you. Many aren't for fear of causing offence. If ultimately the agent has promised an unrealistic marketing price in order to trap you into a long-term contract, they now need to "fess up" and give you the true reality of what the price needs to be in order to stimulate interest.

Sadly, in my experience lots of estate agents don't have the courage to do this. They simply bury their heads in the sand and hope that either an offer will come in out of the blue, or that the housing market will enjoy a huge upward swing to save the day.

What I would always urge customers to do if they're not satisfied with the feedback that they're getting from their estate agent is to call them and demand an update. Ultimately if the agent is consistently failing to deliver, the final option open to you is to jump ship once the initial Agency Term has come to an end (see Step 32).

Because regular feedback is so important, I give my customers my personal mobile number so that they can call me at any time. This is despite the fact that I also commit to calling them (or emailing if they prefer) once a week to give them an update.

Top Tip!

Make sure that your agent speaks to you every week and ask to see the Client Property Report provided by Rightmove.

How to Conduct a Viewing

Remember that before you market your house and get ready to carry out your first viewing, you should have fully prepared your home using Steps 2 through to 5.

On the day of the viewing, always remember to do your last minute cleaning and tidying up. It's always a good idea to get some fresh flowers, nicely scented candles and have some fresh fruit on display.

Make sure that all of the curtains and blinds are fully open, letting in as much natural light as possible. If it's a nice summer's day, open a few windows to allow the property to be nicely aired.

Where possible, try to conduct the viewing during the day when the house is nice and bright. If this isn't possible, make sure that all the rooms are well lit and tidy.

Don't forget, your buyer's experience starts from the second that they arrive.

A key factor in peoples' decision making is the ease and availability of on-site parking. Make sure that your driveway is clear and leave a space outside your house. You want your buyer to be able to pull up and park without any difficulty.

On the day, avoid cooking any spicy or exotic dishes that might leave lingering smells. And don't be tempted to go for the old freshly baked bread routine! Buyers will see through this and view it as a cynical and desperate attempt to sell.

On arrival welcome the viewers with a friendly smile and keep the conversation professional. Don't try to over please or you'll come across as desperate.

Good opening questions include:

•   Have you travelled far?

•   Do you live locally?

This will give you a sense of why the person is looking at your home and, if they live nearby it gives you an opportunity to strike up a rapport based upon your own local knowledge of that particular area. You may well find out that you know some common local landmarks or people, which will help you and the viewer feel more at ease.

If your property has two entrances, you should make sure that you direct them via the best one in terms of its initial visual impact. Normally this is the front of the house, which might display beautifully arranged flowers.

Before the scheduled appointment, work out a viewing plan. That's the journey that you'll take your would be buyer through your house to show off its best features. You'll always start downstairs and it's best to show off your property's finest rooms and features first of all.

That's because your buyer's decision on whether or not they'll fall in love with your home will be made within the first few seconds. If you can 'wow' them from the off by showcasing your home's standout rooms, they'll be more forgiving of any 'run of the mill' rooms that they come across later.

So, think to yourself; what are the best one, two or three rooms downstairs that I can show off first and in what order? Begin with these and if possible try to visit them naturally as you walk through your home, one by one.

It's not necessary to go into a room and announce what it is. For example, "This is the kitchen". They will know! Most viewings only last around ten minutes, but don't be worried if it takes longer. If the viewer wants to take more time and ask lots of questions, this is a good sign of their keen interest.

After the guided tour, you may offer them the option of looking around on their own. If they start getting into questions about the property's features, this is a really good signal of their interest. You can at this point offer them a tea or coffee so that you can continue to chat in a more relaxed manner.

Your would be buyer may then start to ask questions, like "When are you looking to move by?" or "How negotiable are you on the price?". These are fantastic buying signals.

The viewer's contact details will normally have been taken by the estate agent, but if this isn't the case, ask them for their name and phone number so that your agent can follow-up with them for feedback. You should also make a note of anything that they've told you about their current housing situation. This will include whether they're a first-time buyer, they've got a house to sell and when they're looking to move. Remember that viewers are not always open and honest about their position. They want to keep their cards close to their chest to enable them to negotiate the price directly with the estate agent afterwards.

Feedback on how the viewing went to your agent and request that they follow up. Lots of estate agents offer an accompanied viewing service and they'll be able to take care of the viewing for you.

Many homeowners find the viewing difficult and awkward and buyers similarly report this experience. That's why I recommend that the agent should personally conduct your viewings, as you'll understand further in the next step.

Accompanied Viewings

Research has shown that a seller has got a far higher chance of selling a property when the estate agent carries out accompanied viewings. Some estate agents estimate this to be as high as doubling your prospects of success.

Given that it's widely accepted within the industry to be the best way of selling a home, why do lazy agents prefer to sit in their comfy chairs, playing solitaire on their computer, rather than doing the hard work and selling their customer's home for them? I can never understand this.

So, let's explore why it's always better for an agent to carry out accompanied viewings. First of all, an estate agent who hasn't been able to screen out potential time wasters prior to the viewing has a much better opportunity of doing so in the flesh. They can tune into buying clues, or time waster signals. They can enthuse and encourage warm prospects and quickly flush out the 'tyre kickers'.

When a buyer views your home, they'll feel awkward asking questions that they fear might offend you. They'll be reluctant to ask questions concerning the price, particularly if they're looking to put forward an offer some way below the asking price.

When your buyer initially views your home, they'll either decide it's the right house for them or quickly dismiss it. This view, based upon their first impression will be a decision of the heart. They'll 'know' instinctively that "This is the house of my dreams". That's why it's so important to carry out a viewing plan and begin by showing off your home's best features, as discussed in the previous step.

The saying goes within the world of sales that "People buy on emotion and then justify their decision with logic". It's a good estate agent's job to pick up on these clues, strike up a rapport with the viewer and then inspire them to make an offer to buy.

For example, if a would be buyer is looking at a family home and mentions that they have children, a good agent could start to ask about their ages and then point out the nearby parks, fantastic schools and their glowing OFSTED reports. If a potential purchaser mentions that they have difficulty with mobility and lifting, it might not be the best idea to highlight the enormous garden that needs lots of regular maintenance.

After your viewer has been and decided that your house is the home for them, they'll probably arrange a second viewing. They'll realise that this is an enormous decision, with significant financial implications. They want to make sure that, having decided with their heart, this is the right choice for them. They now need their head to justify the logic of the decision. So by the time of the second viewing, the buyer is looking for reasons not to buy!

It's therefore crucial that the agent who conducted the first viewing, is aware of what's important to the buyer and who has already built up a relationship, can attend and, where necessary overcome any potential objections.

For example, a buyer with a young family may deem a large garden to be important, but what if your home doesn't have one? This can be overcome by pointing out that there is a nearby playground or park that will be perfect for their kids to play in.

Another person might bemoan the fact that, whilst the house is fantastic, they need a study. A good agent could suggest that the large attic space, which isn't currently utilised, could easily be converted with the use of some simple loft ladders. By creating an additional functional area, this could in turn increase the property's value. A negative has now been transformed into a positive.

When it comes to the crucial moment and deciding upon the right level of offer to put forward, buyers will always be worried that they might be paying over the odds. They may have seen other properties, possibly not as appealing as yours, but at a lower price. Every buyer wants to get the best house, but at the same price as the ones that are not so good!

Here a good agent who knows the local market can point out the relevant facts and figures of recent sales. By doing so, they can easily put a buyer's mind at rest. Ultimately, if a buyer has found their dream home, they're not going to be looking anywhere else. That's so long as you can reassure them with the true facts behind their decision.

During the second viewing the potential buyer will be talking about their plans and how they'll be going about carrying out major changes. They might want to rip out kitchens or bathrooms, or make wholesale changes to the décor. The occupier, who is currently living in the home and sees it as their pride and joy, can easily take offence. An estate agent who understands that each buyer will want to stamp their own personality onto a house to make it their home, can talk to them objectively and without any emotion. They'll be able to understand the situation from each party's perspective.

When it comes to putting forward an offer, a seller might be offended, particularly if the initial offer is a lot lower than they were anticipating.

Here it's important to remember that the marketing price of the house is not a statement of its value.

The market value is what a willing buyer and a willing seller are prepared to agree. An estate agent will understand that many buyers will look to pay slightly under the asking price. It's important that you set your expectations properly so that you're not disappointed or offended with a lower offer.

Based upon Hometrack survey results, in a buoyant market, for example during the period before the last housing slump, average sale prices were at or about 95% of the asking price. When the market drops, as it did after 2008, the prices achieved averaged between 90-95% of the asking price.

As of July 2017, Hometrack reported the market was performing well with prices achieving around 97%. An offer of around 97% of your asking price is not at all unusual. Whether or not you can ultimately achieve more or less will depend upon the conditions of the prevailing local housing market and of course how much your buyer really wants your home.

Buyers are aware that this is a negotiation process and will often be willing to pay more than their initial offer. The offer is not meant as an insult, but simply part and parcel of the sales bartering process.

A good agent will be able to negotiate back and forth and give sensible advice to a seller. They'll hopefully be able to reach an acceptable middle ground that suits both parties.

Accompanied viewings also help elicit offers, where otherwise a buyer might have been put off making a proposal. They might think that their offer is way too low to consider, so it's not even worth putting forward. That's not always the case and any offer is better than no offer. A seller can always say no.

Often when an offer is put forward, the buyer starts off a process in which they come to emotionally see themselves living in the home and then they start making plans. They begin to see past any other houses and potential problems and they only see ways of getting around them.

Once a buyer has committed to a decision to purchase, a good agent can negotiate the price up through talking to them and potentially brokering a compromise. For example, they may reply to a bidder, "My customer cannot accept your current offer, but they are willing to make a large concession by reducing the price to £X. And in doing so they'll throw in all of the carpets and curtains. This will save you thousands of pounds and you can move in straight away without the hassle of having to source them yourself."

Hopefully you can see that there are lots of benefits of getting your agent to carry out accompanied viewings. My firm advice is to only use an estate agent who provides this service for you as part of their standard sales procedure.

You should make sure that the person who carries out the accompanied viewings is the same person who originally carried out the appraisal on your home and prepared the marketing description. This guarantees the consistency of the message that your buyers will get and they'll know your property inside out. The agent will then be ideally placed to eulogise to would-be buyers about all of your home's amazing features.

By having the same person from beginning to end, you can also get immediate feedback from viewers. This allows you to assess any changes that you might want to make in your marketing, or the presentation of your property. This immediate feedback cannot be underestimated and it gives you the opportunity to respond in order to secure your ultimate goal of a sale.

Top Tip!

It's estimated that you'll double your chances of getting an offer on your home by using an agent to carry out your viewings. It's vital that you only choose an estate agent who provides accompanied viewings as standard.

Step 29

Understanding your Buyer

When showing a buyer around during a viewing, lots of sellers can fall into the trap of wanting to set out all of their property's features, but forgetting that the buyer might be interested in the house for entirely different reasons. What's important to the buyer is the most important factor. That's why you should look to pick up buying clues, such as why they're looking to move and what they like about your home in particular.

Generally speaking people will look at a house because it's in a certain area, but why? Is it because the property is in a desirable part of town, is it because it's near a local school, or is it convenient for the buyer's place of work? During the viewing, if you can introduce questions such as "Why is it you're looking to move?" you can pick up signals to help you position and promote certain aspects of the house. This ideally will be aligned with what is most important to the buyer. The same applies to aspects of the house that you may want to play down. A buyer may be looking to move because they wish to take things easy. In this instance, highlighting the enormous gardens and the potential maintenance up keep is not something that's going to be particularly appealing.

On the other hand, if they have children or pets, the garden is a fantastic area to promote, given its amenity and great use during summer. You can relate stories to them about how much you've enjoyed using it for entertaining, or as a place for the children to play safely.

Families with children place great importance on good quality local schools. Are there any good schools nearby? Do they have excellent OFSTED reports? Do you have friends whose children might go to these schools? If so, you can relate any personal experiences to the buyer and expand upon how good the school is. If it's in a catchment area of a particularly high demand school, this is a massive selling point. Some people will do anything to get their child into the best school and will see this as being of far more importance than, for example, a fantastic kitchen. The kitchen can be changed, but the one time chance to get little William into the most popular school can't.

A house buyer may need to commute to work, to/from school runs and for recreation. Access to local motorways, public transport and nearby towns need to be promoted. If you know from your own experience that it only takes five minutes to get onto the nearest motorway and then you're 15 minutes away from the nearest big city, these things are great to point out. It helps to overcome any concerns that a buyer might have.

A great website for you to do some research on your local area and give you lots of relevant information is:

www.propertydetective.com

Here you'll find links to your local schools, OFSTED reports, census data and much, much more. When you enter your postcode, it gives you a whole manner of information.

You can find out the population within your local area, average age, voting preferences, affluence, ethnic groups and even the travel times to and from local schools.

It's a gold mine of useful information and I'd highly recommend that you use it to check out your home right now.

When it comes to selling your home, do your homework and have the facts and figures to hand in respect of the key things that buyers are likely to want to know. In the main, these are: Amenities, schools for children, commuter links and the best features of your home.

Top Tip!

Check out this website and find out lots of useful information about your local area that you can pass on to your buyers:

www.propertydetective.com

Negotiating the Best Price

The key to getting the best price is making sure that you get your marketing price right from the off. You must pitch your house price properly when it first comes onto the market. See Steps 11 and 13.

The golden rule here is don't be tempted to be greedy and risk over pricing your home. If your house is pitched way above the market value, it will get very little interest. You could end up having to significantly lower the price in order to try and stimulate demand. This could well mean that you get less than the optimum price for your property when compared to listing it on the market at a more realistic price from day one.

When it comes to trying to work out the correct marketing price for your home, estate agents are likely to give you varying figures. Ultimately all of these are no more than an opinion and a marketing guide. At the end of the day, the market will decide. This boils down to what a willing buyer is prepared to pay and what you're prepared to accept. The same house, with a different seller and a different buyer will, in all likelihood, sell for a different price...

When it comes to negotiating, determining the true worth of your home and trying to achieve the best price, it's important to make sure that you've got a good understanding of local market sales comparables. That's houses of a similar type to yours that have sold recently in your area. More details can be found at Step 11

'Getting Your Market Appraisal'.

The best tip on how to achieve the optimum price is quite simply to get as much interest in your home quickly as possible. That means presenting it fantastically, deploying brilliant marketing and exposing it to all of the major property portals.

As set out at Step 25, the first 14 days is likely to be the best time to generate the most interest and utilising open viewings is a great way to stimulate offers. When people come to see your home and see others looking over it admiringly, they'll subconsciously think that the house must be good, because there are so many people here to view it.

Then their competitive instincts will set in, combined with their fear of loss. This will encourage them to firm up their interest with an offer.

Hopefully you'll get more than one offer. Having two or more offers is a great way of negotiating between the parties to drive up the price and achieve the maximum.

Please note - You cannot make up an offer, or suggest that there has been a higher price put forward, if in reality one doesn't exist. When it comes to deciding upon whether or not to accept an offer, this is when it becomes a game of high-stakes poker. You'll have in your mind the price for which you're prepared to sell and the buyer has a price that they're willing to pay. Unfortunately, neither of you can see each others hands, so that's when the brinksmanship sets in.

Instinctively your buyer will put forward their first offer, which is likely to be for an amount less than they'll ultimately be prepared to pay. That's even though they'll quite often confidently say that it's their maximum offer…

Don't let emotion set in or be offended by the first offer. Understand that this is simply part and parcel of the process.

A good agent can then seek your instructions and find out your views on whether or not you want to accept or return with a counter proposal.

Rather than simply turning down an offer, my recommendation is to always go back with a counter proposal, slightly higher than the amount that you're ultimately willing to accept. The reason for this is that your buyer will still like to think that they've got a bargain and they're likely to come back to you with another proposal, slightly lower than your response.

All being well, by now you'll be reaching somewhere close to what you and the buyer are looking to achieve as an acceptable price. If the buyer's proposal is still some way short of what you want to achieve, you can try and sweeten the deal by including some furnishings and fittings. For example, agreeing to leave behind carpets, curtains and certain furniture, which may have a significant cost as new, but negligible in terms of their value to you when you move on.

This will save the buyer money, reduce their costs and make them feel as though they've 'won' in terms of the negotiation process.

Everybody likes to feel as though they've come out with a great outcome from a sale. When both sides are happy and believe that they've secured a good deal, that's normally when the right price has been found. That's why it's always good to set your marketing price slightly higher than other recent house sales. This will allow you some room to negotiate and give the buyer a satisfying glow when they believe that they've obtained a good deal.

When negotiating the price, always remember that you can become too focused on squeezing out every last penny, when ultimately the main goal is moving into your next home. You may feel as though the offer put forward is slightly low, but you have to remember that this could be compensated by you receiving a similar discount on your next house.

So, when considering offers, always keep in mind the end game. It's for you to achieve a sale and move into your dream home. Don't get too fixated by any small margin of difference between an offer and what you ultimately want to achieve.

Top Tip!

If you get an offer slightly less than your asking price, you can compensate for this by negotiating a similar discount on your new home.

Changing Estate Agents

Hopefully your choice of estate agent will prove successful, you'll secure a quick sale and enjoy an excellent customer experience.

If you do have any doubts about your agent, or alarming concerns from day one, remember you always have a 14-day cooling off period (see Step 20). This only applies when the sale agreement has been signed at your home. If your property hasn't sold and you've become dissatisfied with your current agent, you may want to switch.

This is the often the case when viewings have dried up and the agent has long since stopped phoning you with updates.

The key thing to remember here is that you'll be locked into the contract for an initial minimum period. This is the Agency Term and will be set out in the terms and conditions. This is fully explained at Step 20 and you can see my example contract in Appendix 1.

You can cancel your contract after the initial period ends. The agreement will specify how, but normally it's a case of giving 14 days' notice in writing.

A large percentage of vendors do switch agents after the initial term and there's good reason for doing so.

In fact, if your viewings have dried up and you're confident that the house has been marketed at the correct price, it's generally always a good option to switch agents.

Here are a few of the benefits:

1. Your previous agent may have mentally given up and is simply focusing their attention on getting new property listings

2. After your property has been listed, it can appear further and further down the portal search results, the longer it has been on the market.
   That's because portals allow people to search based upon when the property was first listed

3. If you move to a new estate agent, you'll appear fresh to the market and at the top of the most recent listing searches

4. You'll reappear on property alerts, set up by anybody looking for your type of property in your area

5. A new description and new photographs can reinvigorate your marketing, encouraging people who've previously dismissed your property to take another look

6. Your house may have failed to sell because you were unwittingly caught in the estate agency trap. That's choosing an agent who overvalued your home with broken promises that they'd quickly secure a sale – see Step 11 'Getting Your Market Appraisal' and Step 13 'Pitching Your House Price'.

By re-listing, you can re-evaluate the price and pitch it correctly in order to stimulate the correct level of interest.

Cancelling your estate agency contract may appear daunting and you're likely to meet resistance from your current agent who has done nothing for weeks. You're now likely to be met with a flurry of activity and new promises. Because it can be quite intimidating, you need to make sure that the emotion and human element is removed. Simply ask your new agent to take care of this for you.

I have a simple pro-forma document that I use with my clients. I obtain their signature, complete all of the relevant details and submit it to their current agent on their behalf. You can see the wording at Appendix 2.

One thing to remember here is that if you switch agents while you're still within the minimum period of your Agency Term, you may be liable to pay dual estate agency fees. You must make sure that your minimum term has ended. It's a good idea to ask your new estate agent to double-check this for you.

Top Tip!

If your home sale has not gone to plan and you're not happy with your current agent, switching to a new agent can give your property a new lease of life, resulting in a boost in the level of interest.

Step 32

Other Options to Selling

Most people simply consider the conventional route of selling a house, releasing the cash and then using the proceeds towards the purchase of their new home. But if you're struggling to sell or looking at alternatives, there are a number of options that you could consider.

Part Exchange

If you're looking to move into a new build home, you can often benefit from their part-exchange schemes. Developers have large amounts of profit built into each house that they sell. They'll always be willing to move properties on to enable them to close down a site quickly and move onto their next project.

Given their sizeable margins, they'll usually be quite happy to offer you close to or near the asking price on your current home. They do so knowing that they'll still be making a good return on the new build sale to you. This is no different to part exchanging your car when trading up to a new one.

But in the same way that you may be able to negotiate a better discount if you buy a car without part exchanging, you should bear in mind that the same principle applies when buying a new build house. You may get a better deal by buying in the conventional way and negotiating. Obviously, you have to weigh up the benefits and risks. In a situation where houses on the development are selling quickly and you've set your heart on wanting to live there, you may not be able to afford the luxury of time.

As is always the case when you're buying and selling, everything is subject to negotiation. It's worth haggling to try and get the highest price possible for your house when you're doing any part exchange deal of this nature.

Renting Out Your Home

If you don't need to realise all of the cash from your sale to move on, you might want to consider renting out your property. Many people are scared of this notion because of all of the horror stories that they hear concerning 'Tenants from hell'. They're also frightened off by the multitude of legislation that's thrust upon landlords. For a novice looking to avoid this risk, a good option will be to choose a letting agent who can take care of the whole process for you.

The obvious concern is letting a stranger into your home that you've cherished, loved and have a deep emotional attachment to. There'll be ongoing concerns that the property may not be taken care of and a worry that the tenant might not pay the rent.

When it comes to customer reputation, whilst estate agents might have a poor public perception, letting agents don't fare much better! You need to make sure that you choose one that carries out a thorough tenant vetting procedure. I'd recommend that any letting agent you pick follows the same process as me:

1. Carry out a full tenant credit reference, including researching the tenant's previous addresses over the last six years
2. Obtain a reference from their previous landlord or managing agent
3. Obtain a reference from their current employer
4. Obtain their income details to determine their ability to pay
5. As an alternative to a large deposit, request a home owning guarantor
6. Visit the tenant in their current home to make sure that they're looking after it properly.

5 and 6 are by far the most important. Some tenants leave properties behind with rent arrears, having caused substantial damage. They do so knowing that they're normally only liable to lose just one month's bond as a deposit. If they have a guarantor who is also liable, quite often a parent, they cannot simply disappear. The guarantor's home is on the line as security should any liability arise. This gives you enormous leverage to make sure that you get the right tenants and that they behave properly. I would not consider renting out my house unless you have these safeguards in place.

In addition to this, you need to make sure that you get a full inspection report. Mine include digital photographs that are time stamped and geo-tagged. They also include a photo of the tenants present at the house with their ID. You can click on any photo to show the time, date and location on a Google map from when they were taken! It's irrefutable evidence of the property's condition on the date that the tenant moved in.

If you want to consider renting, it's important to make sure that you take out landlords' insurance. This protects you against any personal injury claims from the tenant or their visitors, as well as covering the building structure. You must make sure that you inform your mortgage lender of your intention to rent out the property and that they give you consent to let. Some lenders may charge a fee, or a slightly higher mortgage rate for the privilege.

Re-Financing Your Home

The beauty of renting out your home is that it gives you the option of raising capital finance, instead of just simply relying on a sale. When a property is being used for letting purposes, you can ordinarily re-mortgage it for up to 80% of its market value, using a variety of buy-to-let lenders.

One of my colleagues in EweMove helped his client in this way. They had a lovely bungalow that had no mortgage and were looking to downsize into a home approximately half of their existing property's value. They had it on the market but were struggling to sell it as quickly as they needed to. They'd found their dream home, which was seemingly going to pass them by.

The EweMove Branch Director highlighted the possibility of using Let-to-Buy as a strategy by re-mortgaging and letting out their current home. They did this giving them sufficient finance to buy their new home with cash. They also secured a further £75,000 from the released equity that was theirs to spend.

They still have their original bungalow and retain a 20% equity. This gives them the further benefit of an ongoing income stream from the profit on the rent received, less their mortgage and management costs. They've also kept an asset that will hopefully appreciate in value over time.

The sellers would have never considered this option on their own. This is where a good estate agent can come into their own by providing alternatives and solutions. As an additional bonus, the EweMove agent was on hand to rent out the bungalow and find them their perfect tenant.

Step 33

Other Ways to Sell

As well as considering a conventional sale through an estate agent you might want to consider other options, particularly if you need to sell fast or if your home is struggling to attract much interest. I've set out five alternatives, each of which has potential benefits and risks.

1. Private Sale

If you want to save yourself the cost of an estate agent's fee, you can try to sell privately. There are companies that can provide you with your own DIY 'For Sale' board and you can advertise your property in the local newspaper classified ads relatively cheaply.

Personally, I believe that whilst this option could potentially save you some money, it might end costing you a lot more in the long run. That's because buyers are generally reluctant to contact private sellers. They prefer the reassurance of speaking to a traditional estate agent. The biggest downside comes from losing out on all of the marketing exposure that a traditional estate agent brings to the table. People tend to choose this route if they think that they could save money. If you are considering this option, I would suggest that you try out a cheap online agent. At the very least you'll get exposure on Rightmove and/or Zoopla. You'd still need to work out the marketing price and do all of the viewings, but given that 93% of people find their homes online, this is the very basic level of marketing that you'll need.

2. Quick Purchase Companies

If you're desperate to sell quickly, you can search online using terms like 'sell my house quick'. You'll find a list of companies who promise that they can buy your house in a matter of days 'for cash'.

In many cases these purchases take far longer than promised and are often bought using traditional mortgage finance.

Many of these companies are unregulated. Offers for your home can amount to as little as 60 – 75% of your property's value. Some of these outfits have a terrible reputation and there've been countless consumer complaints. Some house sellers find themselves locked into long-term option agreements only to find that the buyer drastically reduces the price at the last minute even further. Because they're trapped into an option lock out agreement, some sellers complain that they've felt forced into taking reduced sums.

If you're looking to sell your house very quickly, you could get a better price and a safer service using an auction provider. See below.

3. Traditional Auction Sale

You'll have seen auction sales on TV in programmes like 'Homes Under The Hammer'. Auction companies in your area are likely to hold sales every one or two months. Here private investors turn up looking to purchase houses quickly for slightly less than the normal market price. Normally sales are completed within 28 days of the auction date. Buyers are committed by typically having to pay a 10% deposit at the fall of the hammer. If they pull out (which is extremely rare), the deposit is lost and goes to you.

At an auction, you can usually expect to achieve between 85 – 90% of the price that you'd otherwise get by selling on the open market with an estate agent.

4. Modern Auction Method

The problem with the traditional model is that you're limiting your market to 'cash' buyers who can complete quickly. Because your property cannot be purchased by the whole of the market, such as first-time buyers, or people who've sold and are ready to move, you lose out on getting full fair market value.

The 'Modern Auction Method' gives you the best of both worlds. A fixed date to complete with a committed buyer, tied in with a process that allows everyone to competitively bid up to the very best price. It works by allowing would be buyers 28 days to exchange contracts and then a further 28 days to complete. This gives your buyer ample time to arrange a mortgage in the conventional way.

And just like a traditional auction, the buyer has to put down a non-refundable deposit, so you avoid the risk of time-wasters letting you down. EweMove Auctions can sell your home using this modern approach and we're pleased that 85% of homes marketed this way achieve full or above the seller's pre-agreed price.

And the seller has no risk, because if the house doesn't reach the price they've set, they don't have to sell. Our auction partners have sold thousands of houses and this is rapidly becoming the first choice for people looking to sell quickly and with certainty. There is another great benefit too. The buyer pays the auction fee, so the seller saves on the agent's commission!

5. Private Tender Bids

Private tender bids work on the basis of marketing a property and specifying that all bids must be submitted by a certain date and time in a sealed format (secret bidding). This means that details of any bid will not be disclosed to other interested parties. Nobody knows who has put forward the highest bid and what he or she is prepared to pay.

It's open to the seller to decide whether or not to accept any bid. The seller is not bound to accept the highest bid, or indeed any bid. They're free to choose any offer that they feel is right for them. For example, a lower bid from somebody who is readily able to proceed by having cash funds may be more attractive than a higher bid from somebody who still has a house to sell.

A recent phenomenon in this area has been the promise of some estate agents to promote a 0% sale fee i.e. they are suggesting to the owner that they will not charge them anything to sell their house. In reality, they're charging the buyer a very large premium on top of the purchase price. For example a house might sell for £100,000, but with a 5% buyer premium. The buyer is paying an additional £5,000.

I don't necessarily believe that these types of sale are in the consumer's best interest, because what the buyer is effectively doing is paying £105,000 for the house, but the seller is only getting £100,000 of that. The estate agent is pocketing an extortionate £5,000 sales fee. The seller would have done far better receiving the full £105,000 (which is what the buyer was pre-pared to pay) and paying the normal sales commission of say 1.5%. In such an example, the seller would end up over £3,000 better off.

A further disturbing development of this process is the emergence of the practice of charging dual fees. This involves charging the seller a fee to market the house in the traditional manner, but then also charging the buyer upon the acceptance of a successful tender bid.

Where an agent is receiving fees from both buyer and seller, it does raise the question as to whether or not there's a potential conflict of interest. The agent's duty should be to give the best advice to the seller and help them to achieve the highest sale price. Critics would argue that this duty might be compromised if the agent is also on the payroll of a buyer.

Summary

When it comes to selling your house, if you do need to sell it quickly you should be open and upfront with your estate agent in respect of your plans. Indeed, as part of your agent's fact find, they should be asking you about your plans and if you've any date in mind by which time you need to move.

This will help the agent determine the price at which you should market your property. If you're happy to wait six months, then you could go for a more bullish price. If you want to sell in the normal timeframe of say 10 weeks, you would pitch it at the normal marketing price.

If you want a faster sale, i.e. within 2 – 6 weeks, you'll pitch your price competitively, maybe 10% below the normal asking price.

My advice to anybody looking to sell quickly is to always sell through an estate agent by pricing your house appropriately. If you're looking for a very quick sale, you can do this by proceeding with the 'Modern Auction Sale'. This should achieve a flurry of bids and hopefully attract multiple bidders. From there, you rely on the auction fever to push up your final sale price, confident that you'll have a sale concluded in 56 days after the hammer drops!

This should enable you to achieve a far better price than a quick sale company, a traditional auction sale, or by using a private tender bid. Oh, and you'll save money by not having to pay any estate agency commission fees!

Top Tip!

If you need to sell your house quickly, speak to your agent. By using EweMove's Modern Auction approach, you can complete a sale in 56 days after the auction, at fair market value to a buyer fully committed to your sale and avoid paying any estate agency fees!

Step 34

How the Sales Process Works

Qualifying the Buyer

Before your estate agent submits any offer to you, they should first qualify the buyer. That means getting a firm understanding of their financial background, current property status and how they plan to fund the purchase.

For example, an offer from somebody who is chain free and can proceed with private savings is a completely different proposition to someone who hasn't yet even put their current home on the market.

Any serious offer that you consider should be either from a buyer who is chain free, or who has already agreed a sale on their current home. Beyond this, the agent needs to check that they've got the ability to buy your home with suitable funding in place.

This can be through cash savings, or more normally a combination of savings supported by a mortgage. You should also be aware that the term 'cash buyer' does not necessarily mean that the purchaser will have the money on deposit in their bank account. Some people believe that they are cash buyers simply because they're going to get a mortgage and upon receipt they'll then have the cash! The answers to these questions need to be determined before any offer should be accepted.

When the purchaser is buying with cash, the agent should confirm that they've got the actual funds in place. Asking to see a copy of a recent bank statement, or requiring their solicitor to provide confirmation usually verifies this.

If the buyer is proceeding with a mortgage, the agent should make sure that they've received a decision in principle from a mortgage lender. This will confirm that they've been assessed as to their suitability for a mortgage and that the lender has agreed, subject to formal submission and approval, that a mortgage advance will be provided. This will give you an understanding of how much they can put forward by way of funds to purchase your home and make sure that it's sufficient to meet the sale price.

This is part and parcel of a good agents job and will be presented to you along with advice as to whether or not you should accept the offer.

Once an offer has been accepted you're then in a position to move forward with your plans and, where applicable, put forward an offer on your next house. You'll be able to confirm to your potential seller that you have a buyer in place and hopefully your offer to buy will be accepted.

Sales Progression

One thing I should make you aware of is that some estate agents overlook the sales progression side of the business. They spend a lot of their time and effort on securing new business, because this earns them money. But once a sale is agreed, they can become complacent and take the sale for granted. But this is where the hard work really starts. There's a lot of work still to be done to move a property through to completion. There are also many examples of this crucial job being passed onto relatively junior and inexperienced staff, who may not be giving this crucial role the attention it deserves.

For this reason, I utilise a dedicated Sales Progression Team, ASAP. Their only job is to progress, monitor and move forward a sale towards a successful completion. They keep track of the chain from beginning to end, speak to the solicitors involved for the various parties and update clients at least once a week. They do nothing other than sales progression. Because this is their only role, they become highly focused and detailed experts.

One thing to look out for when choosing an agent, is asking whether or not they have a dedicated sales progression team. If so, confirm that you'll be given a dedicated Progression Manager to deal with your house when the sale goes through.

Arranging the Survey

The next step is for your buyer to arrange a survey. Surveys perform two main functions:

1. They provide a valuation on your property that's used by a mortgage lender to determine its suitability for lending

2. They provide a summary of the property's condition

You need to be very careful in your understanding of a property survey, because in many instances, it will just constitute a 'Valuation Report' i.e., it will only talk about the property's condition in very general terms. This is more concerned with its suitability to support the valuation, rather than providing a thorough analysis of the structure. It is unlikely to go into any great detail concerning potential defects or repair issues that may arise during the buyers' occupation.

If you want a more thorough survey which goes into detail about the property's condition, you need a 'Homebuyer's Report', or 'Full Structural Survey'. These reports provide much greater analysis and will cover issues such as damp, the condition of the electrical installations, any matters concerning the structure/ roof and other potential problems that the Surveyor believes warrants further specialist investigation.

Following the survey there may well be issues highlighted that are recommended for further follow-up enquiries. Don't be alarmed, because this is part and parcel of the buying process and in many instances is a condition of the mortgage lender's offer. Your estate agent will contact you to arrange a suitable time for access so that any follow-up surveys can be undertaken.

Just because a survey has been carried out revealing something requiring immediate action, doesn't mean that the problem will result in the sale falling through. Quite often it's the case that minor works are required. It's quite normal in such situations for the buyer to either request that the works are undertaken before they complete the sale, or more likely to ask for a concession in terms of the price. The reduction is likely to be comparable to the cost of works.

It is generally always advisable to agree to such a request and reach a suitable compromise. The reason is that the issue will come up time and time again on future survey reports. At some point it will need addressing. Also, you're duty bound to advise any future potential buyers that a previous sale has fallen through as a result of an adverse survey.

Conveyancing

Solicitors will be instructed to act on your behalf in respect of the sale and the potential onward purchase of your new home. They will send you out their Terms of Engagement detailing their charges and a document entitled 'Sellers Property Information Form'.

This is a lengthy document which goes through each of the rooms in your home in great detail setting out what you intend to leave and take with you. It records your plans for things like light fittings, carpets and curtains etc. This makes it clear to both sides exactly what the sale does and doesn't include and is designed to limit the potential for any dispute at a later date.

There will be certain questions that you may be unable to answer, but you can always reply, "Don't know". If in doubt, speak to your solicitor for advice. For example, "Are you aware of any sewers that go underneath your property?" If there are sewers, their presence may be completely unknown to you.

It will also detail questions on whether or not you're aware of any neighbour disputes. These must be answered truthfully. This is a potential grey area, because whilst you might have noisy neighbours, this may be something that you've been quite happy to live with. But if, for example you've been forced to call the police due to rowdy behaviour, or engage solicitors to commence legal action, you must certainly bring this to your solicitor's attention and set out the details in the reply form.

The Property Chain

Connected to your sale, there are likely to be other parties involved above and below you in the chain. If you're moving on and buying a new home, your seller may need to sell their home to you before they themselves can commit to buy their new home. The person buying your home may in turn need to sell and, if so they too will need a buyer. All of the respective parties, from the 'chain free' first-time buyer at the bottom, right through to the person at the top who is selling and not buying, need to be coordinated.

They all need delicately manoeuvring towards a mutually convenient completion date that everyone can agree upon. As you can imagine, the chain can be quite lengthy. Coordinating this along its precarious path with the various pitfalls that can frustrate a property sale can be extremely difficult and stressful.

Regrettably almost one third of agreed sales fall through. This could be nothing to do with you, or your purchaser, but as a result of a sale collapsing within the chain that you can do nothing about. That's one of the reasons why moving home is described as being one of the three most stressful things that you can do during your lifetime.

Indemnity Insurance

It's also worth pointing out that there may be problems thrown up during the sales process which you may think simply cannot be overcome. Quite often, most things can easily be resolved by using a good estate agent and conveyancer.

For example, if you've recently carried out works on electrical installations, or put in some new windows, you'll be required to produce installation certificates. The same may apply to loft conversions or other major works that require building regulation approval.

If certificates have been lost, or they weren't obtained in the first place, it doesn't mean that the sale will collapse. Your solicitor will be able to obtain relatively low-cost indemnity insurance. This is designed to pay out compensation in the event of any financial loss arising as a result of the absence of the certificates.

So the key message here is, don't panic. Speak to your agent and solicitor and they're likely to be able to come up with a practical solution for you.

Exchange of Contracts and Completion

Once a completion date has been agreed, you'll need to sign all of the legal paperwork with your solicitors. This is known as exchanging contracts. Upon signing you and your buyer are legally locked into the sale. Normally a sale will have a gap between the exchange of contracts and the completion date. This is to allow time for things like arranging removal vans and securing the drawdown of funds from mortgage lenders, ready for the day of purchase.

On the completion date, your buyer's solicitor will transfer the full purchase price to your solicitor's bank account by same day bank transfer. This might be made up of a combination of mortgage funding and a deposit. If you're buying a property, this money will be used to complete the onward purchase of your new home. Every other property connected to your chain will be completed in the same way, almost simultaneously, in a series of back-to-back transactions.

Handing Over the Keys

In terms of providing access to your new home and giving access to your purchaser, this will be something that you will discuss and agree with your estate agent or conveyancer. Sometimes people arrive with their removal van to be met by the departing former owner and presented with the keys. Alternatively, keys can be left with the agent or solicitor for collection once the purchase monies have been paid. It's simply a matter for you and your buyer to agree and work out what's most suitable for you in the circumstances. And that's it!

Obviously along the way, there are various potential pitfalls that can arise from surveys or property searches etc. The key thing to remember is, don't panic. Because pretty much every situation can be resolved and your agent will be on hand to help you where necessary.

Top Tip!

Don't worry if your sale appears to have hit the buffers due to a problem highlighted on a survey, search or property enquiry. Most things can be resolved quickly and easily and your solicitor can take out indemnity insurance to overcome most problems.

Step 35

Property Surveys

For the purpose of assessing the value and suitability of the property and as a mandatory requirement of mortgage lending, your buyer will commission a survey. You will also commission your own survey if you're buying a property.

There are three main types of survey, detailed below:

1. Full Building Survey or Structural Survey Report

These typically cost between £300 - £600 and will be carried out by a Chartered Surveyor – that is somebody who is a member of the Royal Institution of Chartered Surveyors (RICS).

This is the most comprehensive report and will give a full summary of the property and an opinion on its condition. It will set out any defects requiring further attention, areas of concern and possible follow-up investigations or additional inspection reports that are required.

Because of the amount of money involved in a property purchase, many people choose to have a full building survey. It's strongly advisable for old properties, or any house that's had recent major alterations.

2. Home Buyer Report (RICS Condition Report)

These typically cost between £200 – £400 and are carried out by a RICS Chartered Surveyor. They will give a summary opinion as to the condition of the property and a house valuation. These are generally suitable for reasonably modern, well-kept houses and are a lower cost alternative to commissioning a Full Building Survey.

3. Valuation Report

This will cost in the order of £150 – £300 and can be carried out by a Chartered General Practice Surveyor. These surveys are normally carried out for the sole benefit of the mortgage lender to provide a house valuation.

They will only give very general information about the property's condition, which is more to do with its suitability for mortgage lending, rather than providing detailed advice for the benefit of the would-be buyer.

Some buyers opt for this low-cost survey, simply to save a few pounds. But the downside is that this survey is less likely to throw up any potential issues requiring investigation that will be high-lighted in a Home Buyer or Full Building Survey report.

Where money isn't an issue, it's always better to carry out a more detailed survey, if nothing else, for your own peace of mind. You're committing to an enormous financial outlay and ultimately it's better to be safe than sorry.

It's quite often the case that the small additional cost of a Home Buyer/Full Building survey can be more than recouped by securing a reduction in the sale price after highlighting the defects to the seller.

Following on from a survey report, the Surveyor may recommend further investigations. When further enquiries are advised, a mortgage lender will insist upon them being looked into further before they'll commit to lending.

Common further investigations include:

Timber and Damp Report
If there are any signs of moisture or damp on walls, this could indicate that the property has rising damp. This can occur when the ground outside is higher than the internal ground floor level. It can be remedied by chemical injection, but it is likely to require re-plastering and redecoration to the affected areas.

Timber can also be damaged by rot or infestation, such as woodworm and dry rot. Chemicals may treat the problem, but if not, it will require the removal and replacement of any infected wood.

Electrical Report
This is to check the wiring in the property to make sure that it's safe and up-to-date. If the wiring is not earthed properly, new consumer units may be recommended (fuse boxes). Very old wiring may result in a recommendation to completely re-wire the house. Remember that this is then going to incur additional costs for redecoration.

Drainage Report
To check the drains which, if blocked may give rise to a potential subsidence risk.

Asbestos Report

Asbestos can be found in lagging and insulation from old boilers. It was sometimes used in textured ceilings and coving, particularly in houses built pre-1970's. Don't be alarmed if an asbestos report is recommended. Normally all that's required is for a small sample to be taken for analysis. In the vast majority of cases, no trace of asbestos is found. In the event that you do have asbestos, specialist companies can remove it quite safely.

Arboricultural Report

This is to review and make any recommendations concerning trees surrounding the site. This can be a case of making sure that there is no risk of subsidence from trees whose roots may impact upon the foundations of the property.

Summary

Remember that it's the Surveyor's job to point out everything that might potentially be an issue for the buyer. Most properties will identify some concerns. This is normal and not something that you should be alarmed about. Where remedial works are necessary, it's quite reasonable for the buyer to request that these should be carried out at your expense, or alternatively deducted from the purchase price.

What you must remember is that the buyer may need to have the works carried out as part of their mortgage lender's requirements. And if your sale doesn't proceed as a result of an adverse survey, you're duty bound to inform any future viewers.

It's always advisable to try and reach an acceptable compromise in terms of any works recommended and paying for the costs.

Step 36

Energy Performance Certificates (EPCs)

By law you must display an Energy Performance Certificate when you come to sell your property. This also applies if you're looking to rent out your home. In Scotland, the report must also be shown somewhere inside the property, for instance near a meter cupboard or next to the boiler.

An EPC is your property's energy rating based upon the highest rating of A (most efficient) through to G (least efficient). An EPC is valid for 10 years. You cannot market your property for sale or let unless you've ordered and requested an EPC. If it's the case that it's been ordered, but not yet produced, you have seven days grace, starting from when you commence your marketing.

Marketing a property without an EPC is an offence and you're liable to face prosecution and/or a fine from the Trading Standards Office. But you can shop around and online companies offer to provide them for between £40 – £60.

Your estate agent can organise the EPC for you, but they may well charge you an additional premium for the privilege.

EPCs must be shown with your property marketing. When somebody is looking at your property online, they should be able to quickly view a summary of your energy efficiency rating. As well as assessing your property's current rating, the EPC report will set out any recommended works that can be carried out to improve your rating, along with an estimate of the cost. This may include loft insulation, getting a more efficient boiler, or changing to low energy lighting.

If you've recently moved into your property, it may well be the case that a previous EPC report has already been undertaken. If so, you don't need to request a new one, saving you both time and money.

You can check by visiting:

www.epcregister.com

On this website, you can search your property address and download a PDF of a previous EPC report for use.

If you've carried out any major alterations to your property, such that your EPC rating may have changed, you'll probably need to obtain an up-to-date survey. If in doubt, speak to your estate agent or an EPC Assessor for guidance.

Step 37

Mortgage Broker

Unless your buyer is purchasing outright with their own private savings, they'll need to engage the services of a mortgage broker. You may also need their help to secure a mortgage for your onward purchase.

Prior to putting forward any offer with a recommendation, your estate agent should check the buyer's suitability and means of financing, before you can decide whether or not the offer can be accepted.

Many estate agents have in-house mortgage brokers, or ones with which they have an affiliation. They do this for two reasons:

1. To enable a speedy assessment of the buyer's financial position in order to advise you on the suitability of their offer

2. To earn an additional source of income from mortgage application referral fees

When a mortgage broker provides a customer with advice and help that results in them taking out a mortgage with a particular lender, they receive payment from the mortgage provider. This is normally worked out on the basis of a percentage of the mortgage advance and can range from between 0.5% – 3% of the loan. Higher fees are normally paid on more complex cases, for example, borrowers with financial difficulties or with poor employment backgrounds.

The thing to remember is that some mortgage brokers will be tied to certain lenders. This is more likely to be the case if you go to a bank or building society, which may promote their own product lines. That's why it's best to seek advice from an independent mortgage broker. They can give you access to the full range of lender's products on the market and recommend the best mortgage for the buyer's particular circumstances, with the lowest rates available.

Given the amount of money involved and the period of time that you are paying a mortgage, a small difference in the mortgage rate could save you or your buyer many thousands of pounds over the years.

There are three common forms of mortgage:

1. Variable Rate

This has traditionally been the way in which mortgages were lent and, as the name suggests, the rate that you will pay varies in line with the lender's standard variable rate. This will change from time to time. Whilst the variable rate is not directly linked to the Bank of England base rate, they do tend to broadly fluctuate up and down alongside base rates.

Banks often face criticism for increasing their variable rates quickly when base rates rise, but then failing to do the reverse when they come down.

2. Fixed Rate

This type of product has become increasingly popular in recent years where customers look for security in terms of knowing exactly what they're going to pay for their monthly mortgage.

A lender will publicise their mortgage rate and the time period for which it will remain fixed. Irrespective of whether or not base rates go up or down, the borrower continues to pay the same set fixed amount and will continue to do so until their fixed-rate deal ends. Fixed-rate deals normally run for between 1 – 5 years, but certain lenders will extend this to 10 years or even the life-time of mortgage.

The advantage of this type of product is that it gives certainty and peace of mind for borrowers worried about mortgage rates increasing. The disadvantage is that if rates come down, you're locked into the higher rate and will be paying more than you would have otherwise needed to.

3. Tracker Rates

A tracker rate mortgage is derived from a lender publicising the means by which the mortgage rate is tracked and charged. It is most commonly linked to the Bank of England base rate. The amount you pay will be a fixed percentage in addition to the linked rate being tracked. For example, the tracker rate may be the Bank of England base rate, plus 2.5%.

In this example, if the base rate was 2%, the borrower would pay a total of 4.5%. If base rates go up or down, the tracker rate will be adjusted accordingly. The benefit of a tracker mortgage is that if you believe that mortgage rates are likely to remain static or go down, you can save money by benefiting from future lower mortgage rates. The flip side is that there is uncertainty and risk. If base rates rise you may find that mortgage rates increase substantially.

Repossessions and mortgage arrears increase when base rates rise, as some borrowers are unable to adjust to, or afford the higher repayments.

Mortgage Penalties

If you lock yourself into a fixed or tracker rate mortgage, these deals normally last for a specified number of years. If you subsequently want to re-mortgage onto a better deal, you're likely to be stung with a hefty penalty charge.

You should always make sure that you check the amount of the penalty and how long that you're tied in for. This period shouldn't conflict with or restrict your future home moving plans. If you're looking to move in the short term, or you're uncertain about your future plans, you don't want to tie yourself into a long-term deal with a large penalty clause.

Likewise, if you believe that mortgage rates might be heading down, you could opt for a relatively short-term deal to allow you to re-mortgage onto a better product when the initial term ends. Mortgage penalty clauses normally take the form of a fixed amount, e.g. £995, or more commonly a percentage of the loan amount. So if you had a 1% penalty on a £100,000 loan, you'd have to pay £1,000 to the lender, simply to re-mortgage inside the fixed term period.

Application Fees

Some mortgages require you to pay an application fee to the lender. Quite often this is added onto the mortgage advance and is repaid as part of your normal monthly mortgage payment.

Given the wide variety of choice, the differences in terms of the rates payable, the fixed term period, penalties and administration fees, choosing the right one is not easy. There are literally thousands of mortgage products to choose from. That's why a good independent mortgage broker is worth their weight in gold.

They can understand the buyer's needs and then recommend a number of alternatives that suit their particular requirements.

Non-Standard Mortgage Applications

Good mortgage brokers come into their own when it comes to making sure that they match the profile of the borrower with the product offering of certain lenders.

Some mortgage companies will restrict lending to borrowers of a certain age, or if they've not been employed or self-employed for a certain length of time. Others have different levels of mortgage affordability assessment, or will refuse to lend to people with poor credit scores. A good mortgage broker will carry out a full fact find and review the borrower's financial position. This will enable them to make sure that the borrower's status is suitable before a mortgage application is submitted.

Non-Standard Properties

You and your buyer may also encounter difficulties with non-standard forms of property construction. There are a whole variety of different property types that are classified as "non-standard" including:

- Airey
- Arrowhead
- Boot
- BISF
- Cornish Unit
- Dorlonco
- Dyke
- Gregory
- Howthorne Leslie
- Howard
- Laing Easy-Form
- Lowton Cubit

- Mowlem
- Myton
- Newland
- Orlit
- Parkinson
- Reema Hallow Wessex
- Wimpey No-Fines
- Winget
- Woolaway

Many lenders place restrictions on these properties and will refuse to lend. Others will be happy to give mortgage advances, but quite often subject to receipt of an acceptable Structural Surveyor's report.

If you encounter any problems in terms your property's construction, or indeed your property's history, such as subsidence, this is where a good mortgage broker can really earn their stripes. They'll be able to scour the market to find a solution that meets the buyer's needs.

Top Tip!

Choosing an estate agent who can recommend an excellent independent mortgage broker is crucial in terms of helping you to secure a successful house sale.

Step 38

Tax

Stamp Duty

Stamp duty is a tax payable by the buyer of your property. This may be applicable to you as well if you're going on to purchase a home after your sale.

Stamp duty rates change from time to time, particularly if governments are trying to gain votes prior to an election! You can check out the stamp duty payable on your property by visiting:

www.hmrc.gov.uk/tools/sdlt/land-and-property.htm

You only pay the higher rate on the proportion of the purchase price that's above the highest threshold and the rate applicable to the price bands below.

On the 1st April 2016, the government introduced a new 3% stamp duty surcharge to anybody buying a second home or a buy-to-let property. As the agreed property purchase price increases, the tax rate payable increases.

Here are the stamp duty thresholds as of 1st April 2016:

Purchase Price Band	Stamp Duty (Payable on that proportion of the price band)	With 3% Surcharge (Applicable to second homes and buy-to-let properties. A property purchased for less than £40,000 will attract 0% tax. For properties purchased from 40k – 125k the rate will be 3% on the full price)
£0 - £125,000	0%	3%
£125,000.01 - £250,000	2%	5%
£250,000.01 - £925,000	5%	8%
£925,000.01 - £1,500,000	10%	13%
£1,500,000.01 and above	12%	15%

To understand it better, let's look at an example:

Let's assume you're buying a property for £260,000.

You Are Buying The Property To Live In As Your Only Home

You pay nothing below £125,000;
2% between £125,000 and £250,000; and
5% on the value of the property above £250,000

So, in total you'll pay £3,000 (£0+£2,500+£500).

If you're a first-time buyer in England, Wales or Northern Ireland you won't be liable to pay stamp duty if the purchase price is below £300,000.

Further tax relief is available for purchases up to £500,000 to help first time buyers in more expensive locations such as London.

You Are Buying The Property As a Second or Buy-To-Let Home

The 3% surcharge is added at every band level as follows:

You pay 3% on £125,000;
5% between £125,000 and £250,000; and
8% on the value of the property above £250,000

So, in total you'll pay £10,800 (£3,750+£6,250+£800).

As you can see from the example, a buy-to-let landlord or 'holiday home' purchaser is paying £7,800 more stamp duty.

As well as a populist move to take income from much derided landlords, this is a policy decision to stem the flow of buy-to-let investments. In the short term, this could result in a shortage of rental stock, which in turn may push up rental prices.

The government's hope is that it will increase the supply of houses available to first time buyers and reduce or cool house prices. We've seen a sizeable reduction in home ownership since 2008 and the current government wants to reverse this trend.

Anybody who buys a house has 30 days from the date of completion to pay their stamp duty to H.M. Revenue and Customs. If you delay, you could face fines and penalty interest. In reality, the buyer's solicitor will take care of this and make the payment on their behalf. They will include the amount due in a completion statement and require that the funds be paid up front, before the sale takes place.

Some buyers may try to avoid or minimise their stamp duty by offering a lower price for the house and then a separate sum for fittings, such as carpets and curtains etc. However, any attempt to pay for additional items are subject to disclosure by the buyer's solicitor and will be scrutinised by the Inland Revenue.

In October 2007, the government introduced stamp duty exemptions for any homes that were built with zero carbon emissions. To qualify your home must be incredibly energy efficient and normally carbon neutral throughout the course of the year. If this applies to your home, this is likely to be a fantastic selling feature, not least because the property will also have incredibly low fuel consumption costs.

Capital Gains & Income Tax

When you sell a home that you've lived in, you're not liable to pay any Capital Gains or Income Tax. That's because the Inland Revenue provides a full 'Private Residential Relief' to any gain. Any profit is yours to use as you wish.

If you have a property that's been used for trading purposes, for example to renovate and then sell on for a profit and you've never lived in it as your home, then tax will be payable. That's because the Inland Revenue will view this as a trading business, upon which tax is due on any profit made or capital gain.

Where the property has been rented out for a number of years and has increased in value, you'll be liable to pay Capital Gains Tax based upon the increase resulting from the sale price.

As with Stamp Duty, the Capital Gains Tax rate may change with each budget. The Inland Revenue will start by looking at the sale price, less the purchase price, less any costs paid to improve the property and associated with the purchase and sale.

This will include legal fees, estate agency costs and mortgage costs etc.

The remaining profit is then subject to an annual Capital Gains Tax exemption. If there is more than one owner of a property, quite often a spouse or partner, then each person gets the benefit of this annual exemption allowance. In 2017/2018, this was £11,300 per person. For 2019/2020 it is £12,000 per person.

After deducting the combined exemptions from any remaining profit, tax is payable at the prevailing Capital Gains Tax rate.

In April 2016, the residential property related rates stood at 18% on the profit for lower tax band payers and 28% for anybody in the higher band rate.

You can check the current rates here:

www.gov.uk/guidance/capital-gains-tax-rates-and-allowances

Rental Property

If you rent out a property, you're liable to pay Income Tax on the difference between the income that you receive from rent, less all of your expenses.

Expenses that can be offset include:
- Repairs
- Finance costs such as mortgage payments (note this relief will drop by 25% each tax year until 2020) From 2020/2021 all financing costs received by a landlord will be given as a basic rate tax reduction. No relief is available for capital repayments of a mortgage or loan.
- Management costs

In respect of repairs, you can include expenses for money spent on routine maintenance carried out in respect of day-to-day living, but you can't include expenditure used to carry out improvements.

For example, if you repair a broken boiler, that would be an acceptable expense to offset based upon it being classified as routine maintenance. Whereas if you added a new conservatory, that would constitute an improvement. The conservatory will be an item that you can ultimately offset when assessing future Capital Gains Tax upon sale.

Rental Property and Finance Costs post 2017

The government is restricting the ability to offset mortgage and finance costs when determining the profit to be taxed. From 2017 landlords will see the amount they can write off for tax purposes drop by 25% each tax year until 2020 when they will have to declare all of their rent as income, pay income tax on the total and then claim 20% of it as a credit.

This could lead to the perverse situation of many landlords paying more in tax than they earn in profits. With the advent of an additional stamp duty and the removal of finance tax relief on landlords, the current government is attempting to use legislation to discourage renting in a bid to promote home-ownership.

Tax Returns

Whenever you're due to pay Capital Gains or Income Tax, you must submit accounts to the HM Revenue & Customs in addition to your other income. This will normally take the form of a self-assessment tax return. Please note that the HM Revenue & Customs has great powers of disclosure and will investigate letting agents to catch out any landlords who have failed to divulge their buy-to-let income. The penalties for tax evasion are severe!

When it comes to tax, working out permissible expenses, your allowances, exemptions etc., can get extremely complicated. If this applies to you, you may wish to engage the services of an accountant.

Many people are put off by the thought of paying accountant's fees. But for simple property matters, the annual cost is relatively inexpensive. You're likely to find that the additional savings you'll make by minimising your tax liability, more than compensate for the accountant's fee.

Top Tip!

If you have any investment or buy-to-let properties, engage a good accountant to do your tax returns. It's likely to save you stress, hassle and money.

Step 39

Checklists

Throughout this book, I've set out a number of handy checklists to help you on your way.

I've pulled these together in this section for your easy reference.

Step 2 – Preparing Your Property Exterior For Viewings

Clear the garden of any children's toys/trampolines etc.	
Clear the garage/shed of any junk/items that you will not be taking to your new home	
Weed the garden and sweep up any leaves	
Jet wash any pathways and driveways	
Repair any broken fences and gates	
Paint any exterior woodwork and metalwork, for example gates, fences, gutters and doors	
Clear gutters and make sure that the roof has no missing or damaged tiles	
Clean windows inside and out	
Plant seasonal flowers and/or hanging baskets	
On the day of the viewing make sure that the driveway or roadside is clear for the viewer to park their car	
Try to conduct your viewings during the day	
If your property has two entrances, guide them to the entrance that has the most scenic visual outlook	

Step 3 – Cleaning Your Home

Wash down all window frames and clean windows inside and out	
Wash around light fittings and scrape off any wall paint	
Wash down all woodwork including skirting boards	
Clean window blinds	
Re-grout and re-whiten all tiles in the kitchen, bathroom and WCs	
Remove any personal hygiene items from the bathroom. Nobody likes to see a used toothbrush, toothpaste or razor when they are viewing someone else's home!	
Make sure that the house is clean, paying particular attention to the bathroom and kitchen. These rooms should be washed down with lemon fresh bleach, leaving a nice fragrance	
Vacuum the house	
Wash/deep clean carpets. A good tip is to hire a professional carpet cleaner. B&Q and other outlets provide these for around £30 per weekend. These are great for reducing pet smells but hiring a professional carpet cleaning firm is also well worth the cost.	
Clean all of your kitchen appliances. The kitchen is the most important room in the house and your buyers will open up your dishwasher and ovens and look inside. It's vital that these appliances are spotless!	

Appendix 1

![EweMove logo] **EweMove** SALES AND LETTINGS — **Residential Property Sales**
Standard Terms & Conditions of Business

Property & Marketing Details

Address to be Sold	

| Type of Instruction | Sole Selling Rights ⇕ | 'Buy Me' Board? | Yes ⇕ | Upgrade to Premium Listing (RRP £500)? | Yes ⇕ |

| Marketing Price | £ | Guide Price | ⇕ |

Sales Fee (inc VAT)		Commission Fee		For example:	
		Fixed Fee		If your house sells for £	
		Minimum Fee £ (inc VAT)		You will pay a fee of £ (inc VAT)

Seller Details & Agreement to Proceed

I / We hereby acknowledge and agree to these terms, have had the opportunity to ask questions and wish to proceed.

Energy Performance Certificate

Agent to supply   Cost (inc VAT) £
Seller to supply   Use existing or property exempt

First Owner

Name	Title	First Name	Last Name
Address	Leave blank if same as above		
Email	
Phone	
Photo ID	Passport ⇕
Address ID	Bank Statement ⇕
Signed	Date

Special Conditions & Additional Services

| | |

Proof of Ownership   Mortgage Statement ⇕

Second Owner

Name	Title	First Name	Last Name
Address	Leave blank if same as above		
Email	
Phone	
Photo ID	Passport ⇕
Address ID	Bank Statement ⇕
Signed	Date

A Happy Sale · Guaranteed

I promise I will do everything I can to help you sell your property:
• at the best possible price
• in a time frame that suits you
• with minimal stress and hassle
So that the sale of your property will be a happy and successful one.
If you are not happy with any aspect of my service for any reason whatsoever at any time before I find you a buyer, you can cancel your contract immediately and you won't have a single penny to pay. There's no small print on this. No tricks or traps. It's a simple, honest promise, backed up by my no quibble guarantee. There's no risk with my "Happy Sale Guarantee".

Agent   EweMove (Area) Ltd (Company No. XXXXXXXX)
Name   for and on behalf of the agent
Signed   Date

For company owned properties, the Company Details should be entered in the first owner section, with the Primary Contact details in the second owner section.

Appendix 1 Continued

This Agreement is made between the Seller/s of the property as named on the cover of this Agreement, hereinafter called 'The Seller', and The Agent listed on Page 1, a company, whose registered office is EweMove, Cavendish

House, Littlewood Drive, Cleckheaton, West Yorkshire BD19 4TE, here in after called 'The Agent'.

TERMS AND CONDITIONS OF BUSINESS

These terms are provided in accordance with the Estate Agents Act 1979 and the Consumer Protection from Unfair Trading Regulations 2008.

IMPORTANT NOTICE – This is a legal document. Please take time to read it carefully and ask any questions relating to the terms and conditions before signing.

1.   Agency Term

This agreement starts from the date of signing by The Seller overleaf and continues until terminated by notice under the Termination of the Agency Agreement clause. This agreement appoints The Agent to market the property for sale on the terms agreed by the parties.

2.   Additional Charges

The Agent may recommend additional marketing activity for the Seller's property and, if agreed, may make a separate charge for this. The Agent will not commit to any additional marketing without first agreeing the costs with the Seller in writing. The Seller must pay the costs of any Additional Marketing within 14 days of invoice.

3.   Extra Services

Prospective purchasers may be offered a range of services including, but not restricted to, estate agency, mortgage facilities, life insurance, property insurance, removal services, surveys and conveyancing services by The Agent or third parties, for which fees or commission may be received. Notwithstanding this, and taking into account our legal obligations, all Sellers are treated equally.

4.   Marketing of the Property

Upon the Seller verifying their approval of the Sales Particulars, the Agent will market the property and the Seller consents and the Agent agrees to erect a 'For Sale' board in compliance with the Town and Country Planning (Control of Advertisements) Regulations 1992 as amended. The Agent accepts any liability for any claim arising under these Regulations as a result of their negligence. The board will remain the property of the Agent. To comply with Town and Country Planning Regulations, The Seller agrees to not allow the erection of any other such signboard. The Agent will not instruct a sub-agent unless the Seller agrees in writing.

5. Accessing the Property

If the Agent holds the keys to the Property, any viewings carried out by The Agent must be on an accompanied basis, unless the Agent and the Seller agree otherwise in writing. If the Agent is arranging for someone to view an occupied Property, The Agent must agree the arrangements with the occupier beforehand.

It is The Agent's usual practice to release keys to certain professionals who require access, such as surveyors acting on behalf of a buyer, in order to avoid delaying a sale. Once The Agent has established their identity, they are permitted to access the Property unaccompanied. Unless The Seller states to the contrary in writing, The Agent will continue to allow professional third parties, such as trades contractors, or utility providers, to access the Property.

6. Offers

The Agent will promptly forward details in writing of all offers received from potential buyers at any time up until contracts have been exchanged, unless the offer is of an amount or type that The Seller has specifically instructed The Agent, in writing, not to pass on. A computerised record of all offers received will be kept (including the date and time of such offers and The Seller's response). This record will be available to The Seller upon request. The Seller must promptly inform The Agent of all enquiries or discussions that

The Seller may have with any prospective buyer, that are not made with the knowledge of The Agent.

7.   Definition of Terms

Sole Selling Rights

Under this type of agreement, The Agent is the only agent acting for The Seller. No other agent may be introduced without the agreement of The Agent, in writing. Additional fees may apply for such an agreement. The Seller will be liable to pay the stated fees to The Agent, in addition to any other costs or charges agreed, in each of the following circumstances:

(i) If unconditional contracts for the sale of the Property are exchanged in the period during which The Agent has Sole Selling Rights, even if the buyer was not found by The Agent, but by another agent or by any other person, including The Seller.

(ii) If a buyer first introduced by any party during the period of this Sole Selling Rights agreement goes on to buy the Property within six months of the termination of this agreement, extending to two years if no other agent has been in-structed.

The seller may be liable to pay more than one fee if:

(iii) The seller has previously instructed another agent to sell the same property on a sole selling rights basis, or the seller instructs another agent during or after the period of your sole selling rights agreement.

Joint Agency

Under this type of agreement, The Agent agrees to work as joint agent, in conjunction with other agent/s. The Seller will be liable to pay the stated fees to The Agent, in addition to any other costs or charges agreed, in each of the following circumstances:

(i) If unconditional contracts for the sale of the Property are exchanged in the period during which The Agent is instructed, even if the buyer was not found by The Agent, but by a joint agent or by any other person, including The Seller.

(ii) If a buyer first introduced by any party during the period of this joint agency agreement goes on to buy the Property within six months of the termination of this agreement, extending to two years if no other agent has been instructed.

The seller may be liable to pay more than one fee if:

(iii) The seller has previously instructed another agent to sell the same property on a joint agency basis, or the seller instructs another agent during or after the period of your joint agency agreement.

Multiple Agency

Under this type of agreement, The Agent is one of a number of agents marketing the property. The Seller will be liable to pay the stated fees to The Agent, in addition to any other costs or charges agreed, in each of the following circumstances:

(i) If unconditional contracts for the sale of the Property are exchanged in the period during which The Agent is instructed, to a buyer The Agent introduced.

(ii) If a buyer first introduced by The Agent during this agreement goes on to buy the Property within six months of the termination of this agreement, extending to two years if no other agent has been instructed.

The seller may be liable to pay more than one fee if:

(iii) The seller has previously instructed another agent to sell the same property on a multiple agency basis, or the seller instructs another agent during or after the period of your multiple agency agreement.

Note - "Introduced by The Agent" includes, but is not restricted to, anyone who has seen the property listed by The Agent on the internet or any other electronic media. The Seller testifies that no party is currently negotiating to purchase the property and that no introduction has already been made by any other party.

Note - Should the agreed sale price be higher or lower than the example shown in the Property & Marketing Details section over, your commission fee will be correspondingly higher or lower.

8. The Agent recommends that The Seller check the terms of any previous agency contract to safeguard against a potential obligation to pay two fees.

9. Termination of the Agency Agreement

Either party can terminate this agreement by giving 14 days notice in writing. The Seller will be responsible to make payment of any fees due within 14 days of giving such notice.

10. EPC Provision

Marketing cannot commence before an Energy Performance Certificate (EPC) has been commissioned. The Seller agrees to either commission or provide a valid EPC for the Property.

11. Letting

If the Property is let to a tenant that we introduce, The Seller will pay a tenant find fee equivalent to one month's full rent, due on the tenancy start date.

12. Personal Interest

We must by law disclose to prospective purchasers any business or family relationships which you may have with us, any employee of ours or any company associated with us. If you are aware of any such relationship please give details below:

13.   Unoccupied Property

We are not responsible for the maintenance or repair of your property if it is unoccupied unless we have agreed otherwise in writing. It is your responsibility to ensure that mains services are turned off, water, heating systems, professionally drained down and the insurers notified.

14.   Complaints and The Property Ombudsman

If you believe you have a grievance, please write in the first instance to your Branch Director at; EweMove, Cavendish House, Littlewood Drive, Cleckheaton BD19 4TE. You will receive an acknowledgment in 3 working days and a full written response within 15 working days of the acknowledgement.
A copy of our complaints handling procedure can be downloaded here - bit.ly/ewesorry

The Agent is a member of TPOS (The Property Ombudsman Scheme) and follows the TPOS Code of practice. The Seller agrees that The Agent may give information about the sale of The Seller's Property to the Ombudsman, if The Seller has registered a complaint and they ask for that information. The Seller also agrees to allow The Agent to share information with TPOS to allow them to monitor and improve performance. The TPOS code and Consumer Guide can be found at www.tpos.co.uk

The Property Ombudsman, 43-55 Milford Street, Salisbury, Wiltshire, SP1 2BP. Call 01722 333306 or email admin@tpos.co.uk

15.   New Services - Data Protection Act

From time to time, we would like to acquaint you with new products and services available through our associate companies, with a view to ensuring that you are always made aware of the latest competitive products in the market place.

Please tick the box if you do not want to receive such details [ ]

16. Money Laundering Terrorist Financing & Transfer of Funds Regulations 2017

We must by law carry out checks on the Seller to confirm their identity.

17. Notice of Right to Cancel - Consumer Contracts (Information, Cancellation and Additional Charges) Regulations 2011

The Seller is entitled to cancel this agreement within the first 14 days of the agreement, at no cost. To do so, email support@ewemove.com or complete the below and return this agreement to EweMove, Cavendish House, Littlewood Drive, Cleckheaton, West Yorkshire, BD19 4TE.

I/We hereby give notice that I/we wish to cancel the contract in respect of:

(Property Address)

Signed..

Appendix 2
Cancellation of Terms of Business

In accordance with your terms of business signed by me in connection with the sale/letting of my property, I would now like to give you immediate notice to cancel this agreement in respect of:

Property:

The notice period will expire on:

Please arrange to remove all marketing materials by this date.

If applicable, please arrange to return the keys to the property immediately this notice period expires to EweMove upon their local agent's request.
Thank you for all of your efforts in marketing the property on my behalf to date.

Yours faithfully,

Customer Name(s):
Customer Signature(s):
Date:

A Special Offer From The Author
For readers of:

The 39 Steps To Avoid a House Sale Nightmare!

Dear Reader,

Thank you so much for reading this book. I never set out to be a published author. At school, whenever I was asked to write a two-page essay, I'd use extra large text so that I could get away with writing fewer words...

And in truth, having been brow beaten and coaxed into doing this, I've actually really enjoyed putting the estate agency world to rights in this little ditty.

And to show my appreciation for you giving up your precious time and allowing me to share with you my innermost thoughts, I'd like to offer you a special gift...

Get Your FREE Hometrack
Automated Valuation Model Report

The Hometrack AVM gives you an instant, accurate valuation of your home, without needing the time or expense of using a Surveyor.

- These reports are used by the majority of UK lenders to support their lending decisions
- They're the most accurate Automated Valuation available in the UK
- You can find out what your home is worth today

"Our client's base their decisions on evidence not opinion. Just one reason why we're trusted by many of the UK's top lenders." Hometrack Data Systems Limited.

So whereas Estate Agents will give you opinions, the beauty of a Hometrack AVM report is that it's based upon hard facts. That's why lenders trust them and they support 80% of mortgage applications in the UK…

And just as it's crucial to know what your credit report says about your financial history, it's as vital to know what your property's Hometrack AVM report says BEFORE your buyer tries to get a mortgage.

Here are just a few of the benefits of taking advantage of this offer:

1. You'll get insight on what your buyer's lender might see about your house, <u>before</u> you sell

2. These bank grade reports are usually only used by big banks and industry specialists. You'll be getting insider information.

3. No fee, no appointment and no waiting for your valuation. It's a simple online request that will take less than 60 seconds to capture all the information needed to produce your valuation.

Don't risk trying to sell your house without one

For full details on how get your free Hometrack AVM report:

Visit my website…
…It's printed on the back of this book

This offer is limited to one report per household and is subject to change without notice

Guide to Picking the Best Agent

I want to leave you with a bonus checklist. Whenever the time comes for you to sell your home, it will help you in your search. When choosing an estate agent, you must look for these 'must have' ingredients. Use it to help you compare and pick the best. Now the truth is that many agents only have 1 or 2 of these 'Must haves'. But with EweMove, you get all of them...

Question	Agent 1	Agent 2	EweMove
Are they on Rightmove, Zoopla & Prime Location? 98% of buyers search on these sites			✓
Are they open 24/7 for buyer enquiries? Buyers can contact us on live chat or phone 24/7			✓
Are they Professional Photography Academy trained?			✓
Do they have no minimum contract term (aka hand-cuffs)? Or a no risk Happy Sale Guarantee			✓
Are they 5 Star Rated on Independent Review Sites? We're trusted by thousands of sellers and are the #1 Agent in the UK on Trustpilot.			✓